Grasping
Customer Demand
With
Tanpin Kanri

*How Seven-Eleven Japan and Ito-Yokado
Created the World's Most Advanced Information System
for Enhanced Demand Chain Management*

D1226101

By Tomoyuki Ogata

Edited by Daniel Costello

GRASPING CUSTOMER DEMAND WITH TANPIN KANRI
All rights reserved.
Copyright © 2002 by Tomoyuki Ogata and Daniel Costello
Translation by Sophia Enterprises, Inc.
Cover illustration and interior production by Candice T. Ota

Contact the author:
Tomoyuki Ogata
Office 2020 Publishing Co.,Ltd.
Ambassador Roppongi 404,
16-13, Roppongi 3-chome,
Minato-ku, Tokyo
106-0032, Japan

Contact the editor:
Daniel Costello
1431-A Centinela Avenue
Santa Monica, CA 90404-2609
Daniel_Costello@hotmail.com

ISBN 0-9717673-0-0

Printed in the United States of America

Contents

Introduction

In 1973, despite objections from fellow executives, a renegade managing director named Toshifumi Suzuki proposed establishing the 7-Eleven chain in Japan as an independent business unit of his company, Ito-Yokado. This was a time when a battle was emerging in Japan between large stores and small ones. For Suzuki to suggest infusing independent retailers with the franchise convenience store concept struck many in the company like helping the enemy. Ito-Yokado was one of the largest mass merchandising chains in Japan and is still with 1.5 trillion yen ($13 billion) in fiscal 2000 sales. The mission statement for Suzuki's proposed company promised the "mutually beneficial co-existence and prosperity" of small, medium and large retailers. The new business unit would be bent on providing support to these small- and medium-size competitors so that they could compete. What was this man thinking?

Suzuki went to work for Ito-Yokado in 1963 after a stint with a wholesale book distributor and once at the company, spent several years in such areas as human resources, operations and public relations. Never was he directly involved in distribution or any lines of the sales or merchandising departments. Given this background, several executives at Ito-Yokado liked to think that Suzuki didn't know anything about "real" business. Moreover, his proposals were a bit precocious for a managing director.

Yet, Suzuki had indeed already proven himself at the company. He championed reform in such areas as SKU (stock keeping unit) rationalization and the elimination of slow-moving products at Ito-Yokado stores. These were facets of some top-down "strong arm" reform measures that were instituted company-wide.

Suzuki's idea was ambitious to say the least. The battle between large and small retailers aside, 7-Eleven stores in Japan would be an improbable success. Any new concept can be challenging, but this would be even more so given the traditions of the retail and distribution industry in Japan at the time. The idea challenged the status quo on several fronts. To start, the company was founded as a retailer that emphasized the type of operation itself. Seven-Eleven Japan, as the division would come to be called, defined its very purpose as providing for and satisfying consumers who seek convenience. Such a concept went against the understood notion of retailing, which traditionally functioned to serve the supply side, not the demand side. Suzuki believed that small stores would be able to build market share essentially by winning customer support, and the key to doing that would be to pursue value, satisfaction and worthiness for its customers, day in and day out. In other words, the stores would have to operate in such as way as to provide consumers what they want, when they want it even when their wants change.

There would be plenty of high hurdles and logistical complications creating this kind of retailing. Nor would Seven-Eleven Japan be entirely modeled after its American cousin. Instead of building stores and finding franchisees, the company would solicit existing retailers to convert their stores to 7-Elevens. Sales space was an immediate problem. It was decided that each store would need to carry at least 3,000 items to meet the customer's everyday convenience needs. And to accommodate such an assortment, an area of 100 square meters was calculated to be the minimum "purchase floor" requirement. (Since the approach took the perspective of the retail customer, Suzuki renamed the "sales floor" a "purchase floor.") So to start, a good number of mom-and-pop merchants had to move their living quarters from the back of their small shops to the second floor or elsewhere. In most cases, non-selling space had to be reduced as much as possible, and there was almost no room for inventory storage.

Then there were support issues. Consider that in the early years, the average daily sales of a 7-Eleven store were a meager 300,000 yen ($2,609) [Editor's note: all conversions herein at 115 yen/dollar.] Divide this amount by over 100 suppliers, and it's clear that each supplier received only a pittance for supporting a store. Under such conditions, there was no way suppliers were going to rush over every time stock ran low. Nor would it help to increase the quantities in one shipment and thereby reduce the need for frequent deliveries. Remember, there was no room at the stores anyway.

The fundamental issue became maintaining a stable supply of items to meet customer needs. If stores couldn't do that, the proposition was futile.

To address that need, Seven-Eleven Japan's first innovation was the pursuit of a planned order/delivery system, something unheard of in the world of Japanese retail and distribution. Under such a system, the retailer and supplier would jointly set the order dates for each merchandise category, such as a certain day of the week, and the retailer would refrain from ordering on other days. Moreover, both parties agreed upon the appropriate delivery times for each merchandise type, so this type of item would be delivered at this specific time and day of the week and that item would be delivered at that time on those three days of the week. On other days, even if the stock ran out, the supplier would not accommodate the member store's request for an emergency delivery. This was the start of systematic ordering and replenishment.

A second innovation was the establishment of, eventually, over 250 combined distribution centers. These are of five varieties, each handling different types of merchandise with different delivery schedules. Milk and prepared sandwiches, for example, began to be delivered three times a day from a refrigerated combined distribution center. Frozen foods were delivered three to seven times a week from a frozen foods combined distribution center. Canned goods and other foods that could be distributed at ambient temperature were delivered three times a week, and fresh foods like bread and box lunches started to be delivered three times a day.

This system allows products from different vendors to be loaded onto the same truck for delivery to the stores and has enabled the company to reduce the number of deliveries a store receives from an amazing 70 per day in 1974 to about 10 today, streamlining in-store operations.

These limitations ultimately forced Seven-Eleven to make its ordering and forecasting better. The planned order/delivery system put the retailer in a difficult position. Stores had to operate with minimal inventory levels and yet keep good selling merchandise, much of it high-turn "convenience" items, from going out of stock. To do that, first they had to employ some of the SKU rationalization Suzuki had pioneered at Ito-Yokado. That is, they had to clear the shelves of dead weight, or what Suzuki called "shelf-warmers" to make more room for the products people wanted.

Again, the challenges were huge. Early 7-Eleven stores carried an average inventory of about 11 million yen ($100,000), yet as mentioned above, daily sales were a meager 300,000 yen ($2,609).

Clearly, much of what the stores did manage to get on the shelves wasn't satisfying customers.

It is in the context of these challenges that Seven-Eleven Japan created an entirely new approach to retail management. The new approach came to be known as tanpin kanri and was built to allow the retailer to identify the constantly changing customer needs at the store level and respond proactively. Tanpin kanri is predicated on a process of evaluating products one-by-one to unearth why some products sell and why others don't. By wiping out such shelf warmers, or slow-moving merchandise, stores could have more room for products that do sell well or new products that might stimulate demand. Like all customer-focused retailers, Seven-Eleven's requirement is to have the right products in the right quantities in stock so as to prevent lost sales opportunities. Succeeding in that has rewarded the company with multiple benefits, including cutting losses and producing remarkable continued improvement in profit margin.

Systems for Understanding Customer Demand

Tanpin kanri is the cornerstone of the technology system Seven-Eleven created. It is also the basis for team merchandising and has enabled vendors and retailers to respond to demand in revolutionary ways. By building a system to analyze and share highly granular information by product and by store, Seven-Eleven is able to create product mixes that are consistently highly attractive to customers. As an indication of just how dynamic these merchandise cycles are, of some 2,800 items a 7-Eleven in Japan carries, it changes about 70% of the items annually.

Obviously, having the information technology to track changes in product trends is vital when customer demand changes so frequently.

With the help of system vendors, Seven-Eleven was able to pioneer several retail technologies that helped the company succeed. In total, its investment in information systems to date counts among the largest in Japan, not only in terms of the distribution industry but in terms of any industry. Both Seven-Eleven and Ito-Yokado have pursued development relentlessly, often scrapping one entire system in favor of something new and better. Seven-Eleven's investments were on two major fronts.

• The first was to build an advanced data-processing system emphasizing order placement, an effort that led to the development of a new and vastly sophisticated Total Information System.

• The second was to embrace a logistics system emphasizing production and delivery—one that would make it possible to "procure optimal items in optimal quantities at optimal timing under optimal conditions" thus responding to the needs of the market.

A Success Story

Today, Seven-Eleven Japan and the Ito-Yokado Group are at the forefront of the tanpin kanri movement. Ito-Yokado, the mass merchandiser, adopted operational reforms in 1981 modeled after the innovations at Seven-Eleven. Although operating in different channels, the retail management styles of the two companies are today quite similar and exemplify the best practices of the tanpin kanri approach to demand chain management.

Tanpin kanri has helped Suzuki too. He is now not only president of Seven-Eleven Japan but also of the entire Ito-Yokado Group. He got a high-level boost when the Ito-Yokado chain adopted his reforms. Someone who respected Suzuki's abilities and management skills, one executive vice president Hyozo Morita, who himself had long been involved in the sales field and whose business acumen was considered unrivaled in the company, got behind Suzuki and set everyone straight. "Let's just try to do what Mr. Suzuki says—without making objections," he declared.

Today, 7-Eleven stores are wildly popular in Japan, as are other convenience stores that followed suit. By 2001, Seven-Eleven Japan had grown to over 8,650 stores, most of them franchisees. Long the largest convenience store operator, 2001 also marked the year it rose to become the largest of all Japanese retailers with 358 billion yen ($2.9 billion) in sales and ordinary profits of 80 billion yen ($658 million), up 12 percent from the previous year. The next most profitable channel competitor, Lawson, Inc., ended with 38 billion yen ($330 million) by comparison.

And in a case of the son begetting the father, since 1991, Seven-Eleven Japan Co., Ltd. and Ito-Yokado Co. Ltd. through a company called IYG Holding Company have owned a majority interest in the Dallas based head office of the 7-Eleven franchise, 7-Eleven, Inc. (formerly Southland Corp.).

Perhaps more relevant than sales, average gross margin per store has risen consistently, often increasing in rate with the implementation of each phase of new or upgraded technology. Average gross margin per store has risen from 24 percent in 1977 when the company first reduced the number of vendors to over 30 percent today. Over the same span, stock turnover time has dropped from 25 days to around 8 days. Average daily sales have almost doubled, and the chain leads competitors in sales per square meter.

A Lesson for Other Retailers

The US retail scene for the last decade is marked by frequent consolidation. Large regional supermarkets bought up local competitors, then they bought or merged with other regional chains, and today, there are just a handful of chains that hold most of the real estate. Drug stores, department stores and other channels followed a similar trend. At the same time, many chains grew larger expanding, renovating and constructing new stores. Yet, while the past has been about square footage and economies of scale, the present is about performance per square foot.

The rush for volume was heavily influenced by the need to compete with the likes of large format stores, category killers, and similar operators with tremendous economies of scale and buying power. Wal-Mart, for example, profoundly influenced the distribution industry in the US, and in fact, around the world. Not only does Wal-Mart offer some of the largest stores and lowest prices, it was a pioneer of ECR (efficient consumer response), supply chain management best practices and strategic alliances with vendors. It was one of the first retailers to work closely with its trading partners to exchange information and automate processes between them. Other retail chains wanted to do the same and enjoy the same competitive advantages from a streamlined supply chain.

Retailers began to install POS (point of sale) systems to scan items at the register and keep track of inventory. They and their trading partners also began exchanging paperless purchase orders, acknowledgements, advanced ship notices and invoices according to the standardized EDI (electronic data interchange) format. Some trading partners progressed to the practice of VMI (vendor managed inventory) whereby the manufacturer was shipping to the retailer's warehouse based on the retailer's POS data. The focus was on the back end, the supply, and getting products efficiently from a manufacturer's plant or warehouse to a retailer's distribution center. Manufacturers, for their part, were also looking backward, implementing ERP (enterprise resource planning) programs and began sharing information with their own raw materials, ingredients and packaging suppliers.

More recently, several other industries have already shifted their focus "down the pipeline" so to speak, from back-end supply issues to value-added customer-facing efforts such as CRM (customer relationship management) and e-business, the US retail industry has remained challenged to be customer-centric. To be fair, retail has gleaned knowledge about demand through the collection of POS data, category management analysis (which among other things looks at how customers shop categories), loyalty programs, and even such efforts at developing "solution oriented" stores. Still, they have a long way to go before they are truly driving a process in which what is on the shelves, what's in the pipeline and what's getting manufactured is based on real-time understanding of consumer demand. In many cases, implementation of such basics as EDI were never started or have dragged on leaving stores, headquarters and the supply chain disconnected. Consequently, there's no clear picture of customer or product dynamics.

The lesson Seven-Eleven Japan has for other retailers is that success is a product of investing in the business processes and technology that allow a retailer and its trading partners to see and respond to customer dynamics. It's a strategic model for understanding the conditions that effect demand at the store level, where the customer is, and to enable a retailer to squeeze out more dollars per square foot and per customer.

It requires a high level of granularity and detail. Sales of each item in a store must be analyzed against local factors that drive demand for it such as the weather, neighborhood events, customer groups, advertising activities, merchandising, demographics, time of day or day of week. That analysis answers some important questions: who wants a product (customer behavior analysis); when they want it (also considering weather); where they want it (store and shelf location); and how many they want (inventory on the shelf). At the fingertips of a store employee placing an order, that information enables the person to see demand patterns and product movement trends clearly and to forecast and order accurately. Doing so ensures that inventory levels can be optimized, the merchandise mix can be kept fresh, and customers can be satisfied.

The Seven-Eleven Japan story defines the links from supply chain management to demand chain management. That is, from a system predicated on moving inventory to retailers, to one predicated on pulling valuable product into stores based on what customers really want, precisely where and when they want it. While American retailers have led the world in terms of developing systems for supply chain management, Seven-Eleven Japan has led the world in terms of developing systems for demand chain management.

Moreover, while Seven-Eleven's system shares tools common to American retailers and distributors (POS systems, electronic ordering systems, advanced communication networks, etc.) the system goes where many American systems have never tread by leveraging the knowledge that exists at the store.

What is Tanpin Kanri?

Tanpin kanri is a best practice of demand chain management. The Japanese words themselves literally translate to "management by SKU," "item-by-item product control," or more loosely, "inventory control." But such translations belie the essence of the idea. In fact, tanpin kanri is unique enough that the original Japanese term is used to avoid confusion with other concepts.

The short definition is that tanpin kanri is a retail management practice focused on satisfying customer demand through a store-by-store approach to shelf management that employs store-level human knowledge and information sharing about products for the purpose of better understanding how certain conditions affect demand on a product-by-product basis, and then to pursue a cycle of product procurement, production, development and delivery that suits the demand.

With the tanpin kanri approach to demand chain management, a significant amount of decision-making responsibility is given to stores themselves. Headquarters is still very much involved in defining assortments for stores according to past sales and data on customer demographics, but stores have the final say since that level knows better than any other what works in that particular store at any given time. Thus, tanpin kanri does not replace centralized assortment planning or category management, but augments such efforts. It liberates retailers from defining shelf sets according to store clusters—that is, stores with similar demographics—and enables and empowers them to tailor the assortment of each store to the specific conditions of its market.

In essence, the Seven-Eleven story takes us back to the way traditional retailing once was. Local merchants with knowledge about their own consumers ran each store. Such intimacy is invaluable even today. Tanpin kanri, and the powerful, cutting-edge tools that enable it, create a new way for retailers to collect and leverage that knowledge and create new value for customers, themselves and their trading partners.

Chapter 1

Profiting from a Customer-Focused Store

On one Tuesday in December of 1998, as the end of the year approached, something highly unusual happened at Seven-Eleven Japan. The conference of all operation field counselors and certain executives and staff members from headquarters was abruptly canceled just before it was scheduled to begin. The operations field counselors (OFC) provide front-line consulting services to 7-Eleven franchisees and had been meeting every Tuesday since the company's founding. Rarely had a meeting been missed.

The group, which numbered around a thousand people that year, gets together at the headquarters of the Ito-Yokado Group, located in the gleaming Minato Ward of Tokyo for "face to face" meetings. Principally, chairman and founder Toshifumi Suzuki, whose vision profoundly impacts the business, attends the conference and shares his ideas and policies regarding corporate management. Often, his theme is a real-life case study.

When that Tuesday conference was abruptly canceled, it was because Suzuki had become fed up with the opportunity losses occurring from low inventory and out-of-stock conditions at too many of the company's member stores.

"Everybody's saying that the business recession has diminished sales, or that fierce competition has prevented sales from rising, but I think these aren't necessarily the only causes," started Suzuki. "We've been losing opportunities on our own, and laying blame will do nothing to help us achieve good sales results. If you don't believe me, find out for yourselves. Split up and go around to every store.

There you will see with your own eyes just how many out-of-stocks there are!"

With that, the conference was immediately terminated, and all the participants dutifully went out into the field.

Rising to the Challenges

As most readers will recognize, there has only been a smattering of good news on the economic front in Japan since the late 1980s. Banks continue to be in trouble, retail sales have slumped, manufacturers are struggling. It's no longer an enviable economy. When an economy plunges into recession, and as that condition becomes more severe, business owners are prone to become more conservative. The notion that products won't sell well makes for a more passive business operation. Amid such pessimism, manufacturers tend to think, "If we produce too much when sales are down, we might suffer losses from leftover inventory." Then, manufacturers try to reduce production as much as possible, and similarly, retailers keep orders and purchases to a bare minimum.

Doing so wouldn't be a problem if it were in accordance with actual demand or market conditions. However, if one downsizes production and purchasing without truly understanding demand— that is, the realities of consumer need—a situation arises in which there's insufficient supply to meet consumer demand. And generally speaking, since such shortages happen with what are popular items (items that don't sell, after all, never sell out), an out-of-stock condition represents opportunity losses equal to the value of those hot items.

When Suzuki sent everyone out into the stores, he reported later, he not only wanted them to become aware of these opportunity losses but intended to jolt the normally conservative owners of member stores into running their businesses aggressively, not passively, as a way to stimulate sales.

Fighting Opportunity Loss

Unlike a regular chain-store, an independent owner manages each 7-Eleven franchise store. In that sense, there are "strangers" within the corporate structure who have their own interests and demands. The owner at each store relies on it for his livelihood, and therefore, how he is able to run his store directly affects his life. Accordingly, these owners make very tough demands upon the franchise headquarters.

At Seven-Eleven, increasing numbers of member stores had begun complaining that the tight distribution model upon which they operated often left them with insufficient inventory. "Popular products quickly run out of stock. We're losing opportunities to sell. Something must be done about it," they said.

In response to such demands, Suzuki found himself asking this question: How could products sell out when there was inventory in the system? The answer, he surmised, was that most store inventory consisted of items that didn't turn over very frequently or that simply wouldn't sell. This kind of dead stock robbed popular items of their deserved space on the shelf. Denied it, these popular and profitable products were more likely to run out of stock.

He supposed that every single store was suffering from this condition, and that's why he decided to investigate. The investigation indeed brought Suzuki face to face with the same situation he had experienced at Ito-Yokado where stores were full of "shelf warmers." Seven-Eleven could not bear such a mismatch of supply and demand. Slow-turning products would have to be dropped altogether.

Suzuki was quick to detect that times were changing dramatically, describing it as "a tumultuous change from the time of a seller's market to the time of a buyer's market—something that has never occurred before in history."

Cutting Out-of-Stocks

Beyond not allotting enough shelf space to them, there are two reasons strong-selling products go out-of-stock: The first is a misjudgment in order placement, and the other is the inability of the production and delivery side to replenish the store with the item. Solving the out-of-stock issue requires tackling both problems, but of the two, proper order placement is of primary importance. If an order is placed inaccurately, out-of-stocks will be inevitable, even with the best production and delivery system.

Out-of-stocks are particularly deadly during a period of economic recession. The more depressed the market becomes, the more defensive manufacturers become with regard to production and the more retailers become conservative with regard to order placement. They and wholesalers alike fear ending up with surplus inventory and unmarketable goods, and this, again, leads to a spiraling down to a depressed state in which producers sometimes can't meet demand and retailers often miss sales opportunities. Then what happens is that heaps of unmarketable products start piling on the shelves crowding out salable itms, exacerbating the problem.

Out-of-stocks represent a loss of business for retailers not only because they represent lost opportunities to actualize sales, but also because they cause dissatisfaction on the part of retail customers who cannot buy what they want. Since that's what's most important to customers, out-of-stocks are one of the strongest factors impacting store loyalty. And it is loyalty that drives long-term success.

The effort to eliminate these opportunity losses, therefore, must be a priority of management, Suzuki thought. Yet that's not the only problem. The other is depreciation from price concessions that occur when the price of an unmarketable item is reduced. And when a discounted item still doesn't sell and must be discarded, an even greater loss occurs in the form of a write-off. Such is often the case with food products a staple of Seven-Eleven's busniness. And at Ito-Yokado, it was low profit caused by merchandise depreciation that put the greatest pressure on management for reform. The opportunity losses were said to account for a deficit of 60 billion yen ($522 million) in the apparel department alone. If the company could just halve these losses, it would have a dramatic impact on profits.

So at Ito-Yokado and at Seven-Eleven, improvement to the ordering process became the focus of the effort to cut out-of-stocks and opportunity loss. No matter how broad or deep an assortment, when a store's orders are not processed effectively, items will not be properly replenished and profitablily will surely suffer.

More broadly, if one looks at the effectiveness of ordering, there are a good number of retailers suffering huge opportunity losses today. Many haven't even recognized the issue or begun to consider their own management practices. "What you don't know can't hurt you; but once you find out, you'll be horrified," applies to most retail stores in Japan and probably to many in the US too.

Fixing Retail Business Structure

Lost opportunities have a decidedly negative effect on the operation of a business as well as its profitability. Indeed, the profit decline that Ito-Yokado suffered was due to the fact that while the company's costs were increasing (partly due to social factors such as employment cost and the like), its sales growth—which was supposed to absorb the company's costs and produce profit gains—was dropping significantly. If nothing were done to improve sales productivity, growth in profit would stagnate.

This was a time when Suzuki started making a number of famous remarks on operational reform. One of them was "Business results are the outcome of corporate structure." Another was "It's okay not to grow at all in sales, but we must grow in profit." Interpreting the first remark in contemporary terms, it translates to the following: "The reason we can't achieve good sales is not due to a business recession or to intense competition; it is because there are problems in our corporate and management structures. From this we can logically conclude that if we try to achieve good business results without first improving our lousy corporate structure, it will be useless in the long run."

> *"The illness we've been suffering isn't transient like a cold, but rather like a chronic illness. Medicines may appear to work for a while, but unless we treat the structural disease at its source, the fever and other symptoms will return."*   **—T. Suzuki**

Corporate structure isn't established overnight, so survival means working to improve profitability now. There's an old rule of business management that says that any structural reform that takes a long time isn't worth waiting for.

Going beyond Sales Volume

Among all the measures of business performance, the amount and growth of sales are the most important barometers indicating how much customer support a company has. These also reflect how well its corporate structure is tailored to serving customer demand.

There are plenty of ways to boost sales in the short run. One could distribute flyers and hold sales events. One could rapidly increase the number of stores to achieve the impact that new stores present, expand square footage or load up on inventory, for example. These techniques, however, are superficial. They flatten out and won't work for very long.

A continuous and persistent effort is what is needed to win customer support—creating appealing products, merchandise assortments, prices and customer service. Such a daily commitment to improving satisfaction and value from the customer's perspective will grow sales and build store loyalty. Operating a business that offers customers high value and satisfaction—including systems and structures that make that possible—wins customer support in a way that is continuous and constructive, not merely temporary. In other words, more proactive marketing helps stem the tide of opportunity loss.

> *"Even if there is no growth in sales, the company can still survive as long as it yields a profit."*   **—T. Suzuki**

This is the bottom line-sales alone should not be the objective of corporate management. They are a means to an end. After all, even if sales do improve, a company would go bankrupt if it didn't make a profit. That's obvious when you consider how many Internet start-ups went bust after the initial flurry over their growing sales and market share. There weren't the profits to keep the machines running and the floor dropped out.

Even without growth in sales, there are still ways of yielding a profit. One is to cut costs, as everybody knows. Whenever business starts to sour, company after company starts implementing cost reductions, especially with regard to employment costs, all in the name of restructuring. This is one measure for securing profitability, but it's based on the belief that sales won't improve any time soon.

While the general belief has come to be that a corporation must reduce costs to secure profits and survive in a stagnant marketing environment, this was not the measure to which Ito-Yokado resorted when it found itself confronting a decline in profitability.

> *"Like water from a damp cloth, profitability that is secured by cutting costs in the short term doesn't last long once the cloth has been wrung out. It will just make our operation wind up in a depressed state of equilibrium."* **—T. Suzuki**

Suzuki pointed to another way to increase profits when he led operational reforms at Ito-Yokado. "Losses have significantly impaired our ability to achieve a profit," he said. "This is because enormous numbers of slow-moving merchandise are piling up in our stores and on our shelves. Yet if we only reduce these losses, our profit will double without any growth in sales." At first, nobody could believe it when Suzuki started saying that many of the products the company carried were unmarketable and that losses from them impeded profit growth. "It's the most practical move," he continued, "to work on reducing those losses by eliminating those products."

Taking into account the changes in the times, his assertions were logical and clear-cut. The way to improve profitability is to make more of a concerted effort to eliminate shelf warmers and fill that space with more popular items that people really want. To do that, the company would have to reform the way products were ordered, build systems for enabling these better processes and demand that retail stores play a bigger role in ensuring profitability. In fact, they would have to clearly grasp the trends represented by each and every product in the store.

Chapter 2

The Buyer's Market

At one time, the general understanding throughout the retail and distribution industry was that the more products one had in stock, the more business could grow. If the sales floor and back room were full of merchandise, one assumed that a store actually sold a wide variety of products. No one ever imagined that such variety consisted mainly of shelf warmers, or that inventories harbored significant amounts of dead stock.

That was a time when, if Ito-Yokado advertised discounts in a flyer, customers would come running and those products would sell out before anyone knew it. "We used to receive lots of complaints about that from our customers," recalls Suzuki. It happened most frequently during the period of rapid economic growth in Japan.

Yet, the situation began to change in the 1970s. Even if the company distributed flyers, some discounted items would remain unsold. That was a lesson that some things cannot be sold no matter how much you cut the price. As the world dramatically changed, it was necessary for Ito-Yokado to establish a new foundation for the company and to institute new approaches to marketing.

> *"Eliminate the negative practices of the past, and stop repeating yesterday's mistakes. We are now facing an enormous change in the times, and we cannot view this era merely as an extension of the past. There has been an about-face from a seller's market to a buyer's market."* **—T. Suzuki**

Since some products sell well and run out of stock while others don't and accumulate as dead inventory, Suzuki came to understand the issue being that there are products that are marketable and those that are not. Such an idea may be rather obvious from the contemporary viewpoint, but it simply wasn't common knowledge back then. It was a discovery to understand that some products will make the sale and others won't, and that there are products that, irrespective of price, will never sell.

In times of shortage or otherwise unsatisfied demand, people cannot make value selections with regard to the "what" of a particular item. Instead, they are more concerned with satisfying a need for a basic function. If products function to a satisfactory degree and their prices are low, an active demand "absorbs such products like water sprinkled on dry sand." That's how Suzuki described the phenomenon of featured sale items quickly running out of stock and leaving grumbling customers.

As fairly satisfied consumers gradually started making value choices according to their own senses of value and need, the gap between marketable and unmarketable products became more distinct. Even if a product functioned without fail, consumers still might not see the value in it. People now require that products be much more than merely functional. Individual consumers have begun focusing on "what" according to their own values. Take, for example, the tremendous increase in sales of bottle water. While in the past, water was water, at some point people began complaining about tap water, saying it smelled of chlorine or didn't run clear, or something. And now bottled spring water from Mt. Fuji and France are sold all over. People have begun asking for more, and by the way, they don't want more of the same old thing. Now they want water from Hawaii.

If there are both marketable and unmarketable products among a store's merchandise, they have to be treated separately in the business. This is because they will not only greatly affect profits, but also the frequency of deliveries from wholesalers, the means of stocking inventory, ordering from manufacturers, production, and all of the distribution processes. It is utterly useless to produce something that's unmarketable or doesn't sell well. Such a product isn't worth ordering, purchasing, carrying at stores or storing as inventory. It is simply meaningless to distribute something that's unacceptable to the market. This will do nothing more than incur a loss. That's why understanding demand is so important.

These new times inevitably drove innovation in the production and delivery systems of Seven-Eleven as it adjusted to what customers want.

End of the Seller's Market

The seller's market was an era that can be defined as when demand always exceeded supply. And for that, sellers enjoyed a certain advantage. It was a time when production, delivery and sales activities could all be viewed according to the self-centered logic of the supply side. I like to describe it as a time when business was operated on a Ptolemaic view of the universe. The Ptolemaic theory is the understanding that we—in this case the producers, suppliers and sellers—were at the center of the universe, and that everything else (namely, customers) revolves around us. Accordingly, when a producer, supplier or retailer took a certain action, it was in reference to his or her own value judgments:

- Will it bring me advantages or disadvantages?
- Will it produce a loss or gain for me?
- What efficiencies or productivity will it provide me?
- What about the labor or associated cost I would face?
- Will it be worth the effort?
- Can I do it as an extension of my legacy systems and structures?
- How much risk will I be exposed to?

Everything was examined from the seller's point of view, and the seller imposed his thinking on the customer. This seller's market has continued until recently, with a few exceptions, since the dawn of history. Whether they were products or services, demands had consistently and chronically been above supplies, resulting in shortages.

Alternatively, compare that to business based on a Copernican theory, in which all value judgments are centered on the demand side, the customer. The questions one asks change:

- If I were to do this, what would the customer think about it?
- Would it bring satisfaction or value to the customer?

Eventually, such buyer's market has come to mean for retailers consistently putting themselves in the customer's shoes. Once you stand on the Copernican business principle, as I describe it, it becomes natural that you begin reviewing, reexamining, reconstructing and reworking your existing structures of production, distribution, delivery, merchandise assortment and sales. This is the fundamental philosophy behind the operational reforms of Ito-Yokado, the management of Seven-Eleven Japan, the reconstruction of 7-Eleven in America; and the operational reforms of the entire Ito-Yokado Group, including York Mart, York-Benimaru and Denny's (Japan).

Category Demand Subordinated by Selective Demand

Under a seller's market, demand was primarily for "product categories" in the sense that any item would do, so long as it was functional. To use alcoholic beverages as an example, people in Japan used to choose beer, whisky, sake or shouchu distilled spirits, but not specific brands within those categories. It wasn't until category demand had been satisfied that people began selecting specific brands from the category.

So as customers became more selective, some beer marketers' sales strategy was to ensure that when the store clerk handed over the bottle of beer, it would be their brand. The long-time champion of beer makers in Japan was always Kirin Beer. At one point, the company held a 70-percent share of the Japanese beer market. Kirin was more aggressive and enthusiastic than any other beer vendor in terms of calling on liquor stores in an attempt to implement the strategy. If a customer said, "Give me a beer," Kirin made certain it would be their brand that the customer was served.

This persistent use of push sales strategies, including tying in with business partners and using various incentives, made Kirin's marketing power stronger than its rivals, enabling it to acquire a large share of the market. By contrast, Asahi Beer had long suffered from disastrous sales and managed just a 9 percent market share. In a play on words, at one time it was derided as "Evening Sun" beer, in contrast to the company's name Asahi, which means "morning sun."

However, as was the case with other products as the market expanded, fewer and fewer people bought beer without asking for a specific brand. At first consumers began choosing beer by brand names such as Asahi, Suntory or Kirin, and then they started selecting specific products such as Asahi "Super Dry" or Kirin "Ichiban Shibori." Furthermore, self-service convenience stores and discount liquor stores emerged and took a larger share of the market from traditional liquor stores, and people were empowered to pick up the brand they preferred.

Once consumers had begun purchasing the specific products they liked, it became no longer effective for suppliers to just try to push their products onto retailers.

Local, counter-oriented liquor stores could no longer just hand over whatever beer they carried, even if the customer had requested a different brand. Today, when a customer wants Asahi Super Dry, nothing else will do. If the retailer doesn't have for them what they want, they'll go somewhere else. And that retailer may never see them in the store again.

In a buyer's market, marketers are adept at creating specific demand by working directly on the consumer, using the power of advertising to create value and appeal. For instance, a company can communicate directly with consumers how products are tailored to their needs, how they taste better or have superior quality or freshness. In fact, that is what Asahi has consistently managed to do. Today, Asahi Beer has expanded its share to 30 percent.

Eventually such a buyer's market gave rise to a variety of things that were never foreseen in the seller's market. These things have forced radical reviews and drastic reforms of existing business practices. Indeed, companies can't operate as they have in the past.

When Customers Accept No Substitutes

One particular episode serves to describe the dramatic change from category demand to selective demand for single products. It happened not long after the inception of operational reforms at Ito-Yokado. Understandably, in order to eliminate shelf warmers, the company had been examining item trends, one after another. At the executive operational reform meeting at Ito-Yokado and other group companies, another weekly meeting led by Suzuki, a specific product would sometimes be brought in and analyzed regarding why such a product had been created or why it was considered unmarketable. This served for the verification of cause and effect as well as to justify the product itself. In the process, an enormous number of slow moving items were discovered and eliminated at the stores of Ito-Yokado. Nobody would produce, purchase or deliver a product that they knew couldn't make the sale. Yet, unmarketable products were making their way to the shelf.

"Do you think unmarketable products sneak onto the sales floors in the middle of the night?" —**T. Suzuki**

How could this happen? "The only way to find the real solution is to conduct a thorough investigation on the cause-and-effect-relationship and examine why problems occur," argued Suzuki. So an investigation of each specific product was conducted to find out how unmarketable products got there in the first place. The problem, they supposed, was because no one had followed-up on product trends subsequent to production, purchasing, order, delivery and placement on the sales floor. And indeed, they found that shelf warmers were very often created by substitute items that had been brought in to cover shortages of marketable items.

Let's refer back to the beer example...

Suppose that Asahi Super Dry has been enjoying strong sales. And justifiably, stores place orders for it because it sells well. However, if vendors don't carry sufficient stock of Super Dry, or if the brewing company can't keep up with orders, there will be a delay in shipping. Thus, the delivery of the ordered products will be deferred or not made at all. Product supply on the shelf will fall short, and the stores will find themselves in trouble with empty display racks. What happens next is that suppliers will then recommend that the stores carry a different product in the same category, as a means of replacement. Perhaps they'll offer a discount to take a case of a substitute item. Ito-Yokado's investigation revealed that these substitute items were the ones that would later become unmarketable and that would take up space on the sales floor. They weren't supposed to be there in the first place.

Improving the Delivery Rate

Seeing that a number of products delivered as replacements for popular items would eventually become shelf warmers, the executives and staff members of Ito-Yokado had become aware of the importance of delivery rate.

Delivery rate is a barometer indicating whether the exact amount of product ordered is delivered at the scheduled time on a scheduled date. To take a look at the delivery rate of Ito-Yokado around 1982, when the operational reforms began, it was at a level of 50 percent. (Incidentally, Seven-Eleven's delivery rate in those days had already reached over 95 percent. Today it ranges from 99 to nearly 100 percent.)

A delivery rate of about 50 percent meant that only about half the products Ito-Yokado had ordered—popular items, of course—were delivered as ordered. As mentioned previously, it was due to a chronic situation in which vendors didn't have inventory, or where deliveries were delayed. If stores urged them to deliver the products as ordered, saying, "What's going on? Hurry up and deliver the products," then substitute products would be brought in. This was a breeding ground for shelf warmers.

Unless the organization took drastic structural measures to improve the delivery rate, it would be impossible to erase unmarketable products from the shelves.

Improved delivery rates offer a structural solution to out-of-stocks and opportunity loss. However, delivery rates can't be improved through the efforts of retailers alone. Delivery rates can only be improved through innovation or structural reform that is pursued from the shared viewpoint of the manufacturer, wholesaler, distributor and retailer. The only logical next step then was that the company would have to review its overall structure and reengineer its production, delivery and sales systems. It would grow into a cooperation and team merchandising effort practiced in strategic partnership with it's trading partners.

When Seven-Eleven and Ito-Yokado first demanded the improvement of delivery rates, it appeared harsh to the companies' business partners, namely the vendors and wholesalers who supplied the stores. Some regarded it as the selfish demand of a large retailer taking advantage of its buying power. However, as they began to acknowledge the change in times and grew to understand the innovative and strategic intent that the Ito-Yokado Group was pursuing, they realized it would benefit them in the long run. As a result, most of them began to cooperate willingly. In fact, more than a few suppliers and wholesalers had sought to differentiate themselves competitively and positively accepted the demands of the new era, pursuing new efficiencies in their own production and delivery systems.

The buyer's market, of course, implies that consumers hold a position of superiority and vast amounts of potential needs remain buried. Understandably, consumers have begun questioning the "what" of products. That is, what does the product mean to them?

No doubt, today many businesses recognize that satisfying customers sustains their livelihood. In retail, that means stores exist for customers. To put it simply, it's impossible for a corporation to exist, survive, develop and achieve good business results without engendering support from its market. Conversely, when a business or project loses the support of its customers, there must be problems in the way it is being run.

In retail, customer support is determined by whether products, assortments and services appeal to a customer's sense of value. If those products and product mixes aren't attractive to the consumer, the prices will not be paid and the business will stagnate.

Suppose you've found a jacket you like at a department store, but you can't find one in your size. You ask a store clerk if they have any in your size, and she replies they're out of stock and that she isn't sure when more can be expected. You're obviously disappointed. So the store clerk brings you a different item in a similar color. "How about this one?" she asks. But in your mind, the jacket the sales clerk is showing is nothing like the item you wanted. Sure, it's the same category of merchandise, but you don't want just any navy blue jacket. What you want is very specific. There are a number of qualities that you might have favored in that other jacket-the tone, the color, the texture, the collar design, the button arrangement or whatever. You and others like you are increasingly not willing to accept substitutions. It naturally follows that in this era of selective demand, an out-of-stock is a very serious problem.

No matter how hard we work to make, deliver and display products in the store, it would be impossible to achieve good sales if our customers don't choose those products. Therefore, better understanding of customer demand becomes an obvious requirement. And if we could use that downstream information upstream, it would be very helpful. In reverse order: based on customer needs, merchandise mixes are provided in the retail store; based on those assortments, there are appropriate deliveries to that store; and based on those deliveries, there are appropriate inventories and products produced by manufacturers. This is what it means to say that distributors should be upstream in the flow of information.

It's within this flow of information, the demand chain, that tanpin kanri plays a powerful, strategic role.

In a Buyer's Market, Value is in the Mind

Many companies in Japan, including those involved in cosmetics, home appliances and so on, experienced downturns during the 1980s. These were caused by the fact that the value, satisfaction and worthiness of products, as well as the product mixes that the stores presented, had lost their dynamic customer appeal.

Products and product mixes, which weren't arranged from the customer's point of view but rather to suit the convenience of the marketer (or wholesaler), were deemed by the customer to be far from valuable. In fact, customers had begun to see them as worthless—as proven by the fact that in some cases, they wouldn't buy the products at any price. If suppliers had persisted with such push marketing tactics, it would have further alienated customers, causing perhaps irreparable harm to their sales subsidiaries and themselves. Conventional push marketing had to end, and companies had to start taking immediate steps toward the creation of stores that had the ability to pull in customers.

As explained earlier, in the seller's market, functionality alone defined value. Such value was created upstream in the product flow, for example, at the factory or in the field of agricultural or marine production. The downstream components of the distribution channel, the distributor, wholesaler or retailer, weren't responsible for creating value. Instead, their task was merely to take the value that was created upstream and deliver it to consumers at the end of the product flow. Indeed, the distribution end was viewed as a cost center, the function of which was to disseminate valued product at the lowest possible cost per unit.

Moreover, the gross margins of wholesale or retail sales weren't considered to be values that wholesalers and retailers earned on their own; first and foremost, they were given by the manufacturers or producers who had created the value. Therefore, there was a notion that distribution was better if it functioned at a lower gross margin rate, and low-margin management was admired in the fields of distribution and retailing. There were even plans for unmanned stores.

Value is Formed at the Retail Level

As times have changed to a buyer's market, it's now widely recognized that the retail store, where product value or product marketability is created in the mind of a consumer when he or she comes face to face with an item and where demand is satisfied, is the place where value is formed. Accordingly, distribution should no longer be considered a cost center.

If distribution is instead a profit center where value is formed, then retail gross margin can now be considered an added value. In fact, nowadays in the management of distribution business, an increased gross margin rate has become a theme of key importance. And both Seven-Eleven and Ito-Yokado, have enjoyed remarkable increases in gross margin rates since promoting operational reforms. (Chart 1).

At Ito-Yokado the inventory level began to plummet after shelf

**Chart 1: Ito-Yokado Gross Margin Rate
Immediately Following Operational Reforms**

	Index of inventory per square meter (FY 1982 =100)	Gross margin rate (%)	Index of operating earnings (FY 1982 = 100)
1982	100	25.9	100
1983	83.9	27.2	134.3
1984	73.4	28.6	153.7
1985	72.4	29.3	176.4

warmers were eliminated. The corresponding effect was directly reflected in an improved gross margin rate. This was followed by growth in sales, just as had happened at Seven-Eleven.

Whether it's a manufacturer, wholesaler, retailer or any other kind of business, the elimination of wasteful spending and pursuit of low-cost operation is arguably a virtue of responsible management. However, in some cases it's no longer reasonable to hold down distribution costs. Downstream activities have an impact reaching beyond the issue of determining orders and product mixes at the retail level. As that information is fed back to the midstream and upstream of the distribution channel, it also directs production and delivery. Accordingly, it makes perfect sense to throw labor and cost into this field since it's where such essential customer information is generated, where value is formed—and whereby greater value can be created.

While value created in production upstream can be referred to as "functional value," being intrinsic to the product itself, the value created in the consumer's mind can be called the "semantic value," "informational value" or "cultural value." These values are intangible and even for the same person, the appraisals he or she makes change according to the time, place, occasion and scene, as well as with that person's own changing needs.

Such changes in demand would compel Seven-Eleven to change in two aspects. The first would be to do business based on a daily process of "examination, hypothesis, and reexamination," as will be explained in detail later. This facilitates a marketing approach that aims for a larger volume of demand and is completely different from past practices. This is the core of tanpin kanri.

Chapter 3

Inventory and Ordering in a Changing Environment

A couple of problems emerge from the buyer's market that necessitate changing how we do business. One of the problems is, even for the same product, the values created in a consumer's mind aren't always the same. I describe this as "a single item has a hundred faces." The other problem is that the values created in the consumer's mind are easily changed, and this produces a tendency toward shorter merchandise lifecycles.

One of the things we often see in Japan is the so-called "queue phenomenon." This is where a high profile, trendy store becomes wildly popular with the public, especially younger customers, and receives lots of media attention. While popular stores have always been around, it was sometime toward the end of the 1970s that many more began to pop up. But looking back on the various queue phenomena that have appeared over that time, one thing applies to most, if not all, of them—these booms have been short-lived and transient. This reflects the fact that, among people who contribute to this phenomenon, value appraisals change easily.

When this queue phenomenon ends for such a popular store, it isn't because the business itself has deteriorated. For example, in the case of a restaurant, it isn't because the food has lost its flavor or the service has taken a turn for the worse. In the case of a retail store, it isn't because the quality of the merchandise has dropped, the store clerks have become gruff or anything like that. Indeed, these aren't the reasons a store may lose its customers. It may operate the way it always had, but gradually customers simply stop coming.

What has happened is that in the customer's mind, it has become no longer meaningful just to wait in line at that store. In other words, the informational and semantic values that had developed the queue phenomenon decrease or totally disappear. Customers arbitrarily appraise the value of a store, and just as arbitrarily, render it valueless.

The Queue Phenomenon

Early in the 1980s, the queue phenomenon occurred at Haagen-Dazs in the trendy Roppongi part of Tokyo. To join the queue and eat Haagen-Dazs ice cream was all young people needed to be hip at that time. However, this boom didn't last very long. It shifted to another ice cream shop, Hobson's, in Nishi-Azabu, another fashionable area only a little way from Roppongi. Customers had started leaving Haagen-Dazs one by one, and today the Roppongi ice cream shop no longer exists. Hobson's is destined to suffer the same fate.

As much as 70 percent of the SKUs change yearly at 7-Eleven stores in Japan. This practice of constantly refreshing the mix shows an attempt to respond to the mentality of customers who always want something new. Some retailers have described frequent new product introductions as competition against the customer's sense of boredom. In any case, failing to adjust to the times should be viewed as the most deadly enemy in business today.

Why? Because such "pulse-type" product lifecycles are increasingly visible among today's products. Products live fast and die young. Items that have lost their freshness (including a freshness in feeling) lose value and become nothing more than bad inventory. Such items will never sell in a buyer's market in which consumers have begun honing their value judgments. So just as the lifecycles of popular stores have shortened, so too have product lifecycles. Yesterday's marketable products become today's unmarketable ones. For companies trying to provide value, that's a terrifying thought with huge implications on how to do business.

This pulse phenomenon exists beyond retail. The president of an Italian pasta restaurant chain told me it was the company's practice to restart restaurants whose performance deteriorates two years in a row. They do this by changing menus, signs, managers, store interiors, exteriors and so on. When customers get bored, that's it. By refreshing the image, however, the restaurant can draw customers in again.

Music is also the same. Previously, songs would gradually achieve popularity after their release, become a big hit and then eventually fade out as if the tide were ebbing. But recently, it seems hit songs become a sudden and explosive hit and then just as quickly disappear.

It's an era of increasingly shorter product and business lifecycles, and it's just impossible to obtain customer loyalty with old-fashioned product assortments and traditional practices of business management.

Shortening Product Lifecycles

It can be argued that we live in a time with few "regular" products. Although some products like Procter & Gamble's Tide or General Mills' Cheerios have sold well in the United States for decades, they're increasingly rare. Even if a product becomes a hit, it's difficult for it to sustain its popularity. Like a trendy store, a hit product is eventually overtaken by a new product or new variety, as these roll out one after another.

Considering that eventuality, imagine how dangerous it is to carry large inventories. Shortened merchandise lifecycles have indeed changed the meaning of inventory in business. In the seller's market it wasn't a problem for manufacturers to produce too much product or for retailers to carry too much inventory. Nor were wholesalers at great risk if manufacturers pushed a great deal of inventory on them. The same could be ture of retailers too. As I've noted, in those days, the prevalent thinking was that it was advantageous to carry a large amount of inventory. In times of relative poverty—the days of the seller's market when there weren't enough products to meet consumer needs—demand had always exceeded supply, so naturally it was advantageous to carry large inventories.

In harsher economic times, or when supply is short, those who held the products were strong. Even today it can still sometimes happen. In the event that a product or store has a unique value that can't be satisfied by any other product, if the supply continually falls short of demand, a seller's market will emerge as a byproduct of supply-side superiority. In fact, there exists such a marketing technique as to purposely create a shortage. But it hardly works today. Once consumers can no longer find informational or semantic value in a product or store, it's all over.

Functional values aside, with the semantic and informational values created in the minds of consumers being within the consumer's own control, it's difficult to maintain a structure of supply-side superiority, no matter how hard you try to manipulate the situation.

Correlating Inventory, Sales and Gross Margin Rate

The relationship among 7-Eleven's inventory, sales and gross margin from 1976 to 1991 provides some interesting data (Chart 2). As the average final inventory of 7-Eleven's member stores decreased,

Chart 2. Annual Index of 7-Eleven's Inventory, Gross Margin, and Daily Sales

Fiscal year	Aggregate average of final inventory gross margin per store (thousands of yen)	Average gross margin rate	Aggregate average of daily sales per store (thousands of yen)
'76	9090	24.0	365
'77	8730	24.3	366
'78	8430	24.9	396
'79	7740	25.0	419
'80	6890	25.9	435
'81	6260	26.4	463
'82	6230	26.8	483
'83	5940	26.9	482
'84	5590	27.2	486
'85	5470	27.4	502
'86	5360	27.7	506
'87	5240	28.0	508
'88	5100	28.3	524
'89	4950	28.6	545
'90	4800	28.8	564
'91	4800	29.0	629
'92	na	29.0	669
'93	na	29.3	682
'94	na	29.4	669
'95	na	29.6	676
'96	na	29.9	662
'97	na	29.9	669
'98	na	29.8	676
99	na	30.0	678
00	na	30.0	681

one can clearly see a continued increase in the average daily sales per member store and in the gross margin rate. There is an inverse correlation.

Remember, Seven-Eleven investigated the items it sells and its merchandise mixes, one by one, via the hypothesis put forth by

Suzuki: "Why do popular items run out of stock when there is inventory available? It must be because much of the shelf consists of unmarketable shelf warmers." And it began to eliminate its accumulated dead stock of unmarketable items that was taking up sales floor space.

This did more than expose the existing dead stock. By paying close attention to individual product trends, the merchandise mix was revitalized, leading to the return of improved sales.

Although 7-Eleven rarely resorts to discount sales as a means of clearing out inventory, the company does discard unsold items that are past their use-by dates, or products that have lost their value. The losses incurred from these discarded products had held down the gross margin rate. But as the company was able to eliminate such write-offs, there was an upward trend in the gross margin rate.

Store Loyalty

Loyalty is based on an assessment the customer makes regarding a store that's formed through their everyday encounters with the store. The assessment includes image, trustworthiness, reliability, friendliness, and above all, the expectation of and satisfaction of a shopping experience. Depending on how loyalty is affected by these factors, the same product could sell in a number of different ways from one store to the next, which is no small point.

In the intensely competitive world of distribution, store loyalty has been brought into focus as one of the important factors determining competitive dominance. That is, one product can make the sale at one store but can't at another.

And the gap between these two types of stores has widened. If we deliver products to a store where they don't sell well, sales efficiency will be diminished. So, if we make the same deal for every store, it's better to choose a store offering brisk sales for a product. Accordingly, stores with poor sales can't get cooperation from their business partners, and this in turn widens the gap between the store that can sell well and the store that can't.

Store loyalty is, to put it simply, the power of persuasion a store has over its customer. Even among products that are referred to as national brands, which are always the same wherever one purchases them, sales vary according to the conditions of store loyalty. So, in the case of generic or store brands, the various customer assessments regarding the store that sells the product will bring forth many more points of crucial difference in regard to sales. To see it from another perspective, a product that sells anywhere can't avoid becoming the target of price competition, yielding the retailer only a small margin. If it's a brand name product, no matter where it's sold the customer assesses the product itself. Whichever store sells it is of little consequence.

Store brands—which are many at 7-Eleven and include most fresh products such as box lunches, prepared foods, rice balls and baked breads—can't readily be compared to other retailers' products. This can be said for fashion merchandise, as well. Products that are high in taste, quality, freshness, or in informational or semantic value for a certain customer are hard to rate. Price tags alone don't equate to value. This kind of merchandise can be differentiated through the appeal of its relative value and as such, is rarely involved in price competition. Value is more likely to be created in the consumer's mind. For example, people may buy because "it's this store" or "it's that store." The persuasive power of the store handling an item will be the major value criteria that the consumer uses for assessing product value. Store loyalty can make the difference in terms of sales growth, so stores in which these types of products make the sale naturally have high gross margin rates.

At 7-Eleven stores, loyalty is enhanced through attention to the merchandise assortment. This isn't limited to 7-Eleven. An improvement in the merchandise mix in keeping with the customer's perspective can be considered a best practice in terms of enhancing store loyalty. It allows the retailer to sell more products with high added value, which increases daily sales and improves the gross margin rate.

The Importance of the Purchase Order

Whether it's a retailer, wholesaler or manufacturer, the entire distribution business starts and ends with a purchase order. In the manufacturer's case, production decisions regarding what to make, how much to make or when to make it are generally defined by order conditions. For wholesalers and retailers, the purchase or procurement of products that they plan to sell is also based entirely on the placement of orders.

The seller's market was one in which ordering didn't receive the kind of attention it gets today. It wasn't much of an issue then whether too many orders were placed, or whether there were too few. When there were too few orders—that is when too many items were being produced—inventory was absorbed by demand over a relatively long period of time. So, except for items whose freshness mattered, they never became dead stock. In a pinch, most of the surplus could be moved through price reductions. It's no longer universally true, however, that reducing prices will clear away accumulated stock. Consequently, excessive production, purchasing or procurement that results from the low order accuracy causes bad inventory conditions and the accumulation of shelf warmers.

Similarly, in cases where there were too many orders and production fell short, a product could be substituted with another from the same category, and the out-of-stock wouldn't be a serious problem. Customers didn't make keen selections based on value. Today, in the era of selective demand, there are no generic replacements, and an out-of-stock caused by low accuracy of orders brings irreparable damage to the companies involved. Customers are less likely to accept substitutes. They'll be dissatisfied, and loyalty will suffer.

With the advent of the buyer's market, therefore, the accuracy of orders must be a subject of considerable focus, especially given shortened product lifecycles. In fact, it's now the key to successful management.

Product lifecycles used to end only due to functional damage or degradation. Like fresh food, the lifecycle ends for a product because it loses its freshness over time. But in the modern lifecycle, the deterioration or effacement of value, be it informational or semantic, is much more relevant a factor. It doesn't occur only to fresh foods but to most products (commodities being the exception, as will be explained later). High-fashion clothing is one such example of a product whose lifecycle ends from the effacement of value, rather than from functional degradation.

Today, unless you're extremely careful in ordering, you'll have excessive inventory from producing or purchasing too many items. And if that situation isn't handled properly, before you know it those items will accumulate into an enormous amount of dead stock. Soon your warehouses and shelves will be awash in unmarketable products.

When underproduction or shortages of procured merchandise occur due to low accuracy in the taking and processing of orders, the result is out-of-stocks. Those are double dangerous since they represent a business opportunity loss for the retailer and because customers are denied what they want to buy.

"The problem with out-of-stocks is that they create an unfavorable situation for customers, and that's worse than the opportunity loss that befalls a company." **—T. Suzuki**

If such a situation happens continually at a store, it will inevitably lead to a loss of trust among customers and the sense that the store isn't reliably meeting their needs. The store then becomes a disappointment in terms of customer expectations, resulting in a significant decline in store loyalty and sales.

Approximating Demand

A slight departure from the subject here, in order that we can discuss the concepts of "actual demand" and "forecasted demand." Needless to say, decisions with regard to production, delivery, purchasing and the product mix are made on the basis of forecasted demand, unless they're made-to-order products. To put it another way, such decisions are based on the projected amount of product to be sold. If forecasted demand equaled actual demand, nothing would make everyone happier. But in reality, that never happens. No matter how much the technology of sales forecasting might progress, there will always be a gap between forecasted demand and actual demand.

In the era of the seller's market, this divergence wasn't such a serious issue. When there was a broad gap between them, say forecasted demand exceeded actual demand, it was possible to approximate the two through the use of push marketing. Moreover, new marketing techniques also proved effective, including creating the so-called "dependence effect" of mass-market advertising, which tempted the customer to purchase, or the carrot-and-stick push marketing approach, which was made possible by controlling the midstream and downstream distribution channels.

Such methods are no longer effective at bringing actual demand closer to forecasted demand. In that regard, tanpin kanri plays a role in improving the accuracy of orders to grasp actual demand. I can't emphasize enough that tanpin kanri has the most significant meaning when it's used in reference to improving the accuracy of orders.

Chapter 4

Grasping the Many Forces That Impact Demand

One of the main challenges in narrowing the gap between forecasted demand and actual demand is that so many factors are at play. Sales trends of items vary dramatically in accordance with the environment and a number of background factors.

In the seller's market, goods had their own intrinsic value and sales were scarcely influenced by the conditions in which the products were sold. The simple law of indifference applied. That is, the same item was regarded in the same way by consumers regardless of where and how it was sold, and regardless of who sold it. No one in the actual business scene seriously considered the possibility that value itself might change depending on the conditions under which goods were sold.

Still, even in a seller's market, certain situations and sales conditions could bring about variation in sales. For example, sales of an item naturally varied depending on where a store was located, how much pulling power the store had, how the goods were merchandised on the sales floor and price.

Today, however, complex and diverse conditions have a much stronger influence on sales of specific items. Such conditions may influence sales more than price will. Let's examine some of these.

Demand: Varies with Channel

What constitutes good-selling merchandise depends on the channel and type of operation—superstore, supermarkets, convenience store, specialty store, and so on. What sells well in a department store might not sell well in a convenience store and vice versa. Differences in the type of operation mean differences in customer expectations. "Different customer expectations" doesn't necessarily mean the perspective of different customers, however. Although he or she is the same individual, a customer expects different things and different types of content whether shopping in a department store, a neighborhood convenience store, a supermarket or a discount store, but in each instance he expects different things and different types of content.

We seldom expect to find convenience items or discount goods in a department store. On the other hand, we don't expect the high product quality or hospitable service provided by department stores, much less the convenience we expect from a convenience store, from a discount store. It's only natural that, if the customers' expectations are different, different items will be strong sellers in different channels.

Again, I emphasize that the times have changed. In the past, fewer elements competed for the creation of value in the consumer's mind, so the products that sold well did so in almost all channels. In many cases the merchandise that sold well in department stores' food sections sold in large volume in supermarkets, as well. Accordingly, an imitative business, which simply followed the merchandise mix of one or another stores, was pursued and could achieve a measure of success. The idea was that if one were to look at the movement of goods in a department store to find out what was selling well and then bring such items into one's own store, they would also sell well.

Today, those differences in purchase location, inspire product development based on the qualities of each channel and the specific expectations among consumers there.

Demand: Varies with Store Loyalty

Loyalty represents the degree of trust and credibility that accrues in the consumer's mind in the course of his or her everyday encounters with a business, or from accessibility and satisfaction that he or she gets by shopping at a certain store. Sales of a specific SKU vary from store to store, and this is clearly attributable to the differences in store loyalty. It's a reflection of the positive image that users have toward one store or another. Thus it's now impossible to talk about sales trends of specific items while ignoring differences in store loyalty.

For some types of merchandise, even the very same SKU, there is a big difference in sales at 7-Eleven versus other convenience store chains, even though operations are the same throughout the channel. The fact that melon bread sells well at 7-Eleven stores doesn't mean that melon bread flies off the shelves at every other convenience store or bakery. The times have changed completely such that sales of individual items vary according to the type of operation as well as the characteristics, features and personality inherent in each chain and store.

Given that unique situation, it seems each chain and each store should identify and develop its own strong-selling products.

The *Nikkei Ryutsu Shimbun*, a major trade newspaper for the distribution industry, announces the rankings of the strongest-selling product in Japan every year. Lately, not only have the sales of such items become less impressive, they've also changed according to certain trends in demand, rather than following trends for certain items or merchandise categories. This demonstrates the fact that there are fewer big hits or home runs that can sell equally well everywhere. Nonetheless, it is possible to find a number of hit products by viewing the situation from a different perspective, even under today's conditions where goods "don't sell that well" and steady growth in demand is no longer the rule. To identify hit products, one must change the criteria to "what is a hit product in my store."

Demand: Varies with Site Characteristics /Area Demographics

An item may sell better or worse depending on the characteristics of the trade area and customer group. Competitive conditions within the area also have a significant influence on sales.

The same box lunch, for example, will sell differently at residentially located 7-Eleven stores, those located on streets with heavy truck traffic, those near the employee dorms of a factory, those near a junior high or high school, a station, a downtown business district teaming with office people, and so on. Demand for the same product will differ according to the location in which it's sold. In a store near a high school there may be demand from hungry students engaged in after-school sports activities. They may drop by to fill up before heading home. In a store located in a business district, there may be demand from workers who miss breakfast and want something to take to the office just to have something in their stomachs before work. Or there may be particular demand from female office workers who buy a lot of salads for lunch.

These different characteristics of site, trade area and customer group create big differences in product sales trends.

Demand: Varies with Weather

Elements that are far beyond the characteristics involving the type of operation, store loyalty, site characteristics, trade area characteristics or customer group also have a great influence on how items sell. Most of us are aware of seasonal changes to merchandise. Not many department stores sell thick winter jackets in the heat of summer. But demand varies by the weather too. As proof, even in the same store, the same item won,t sell the same way every time, depending on the weather.

Weather influences sales not just for vinyl umbrellas or winter jackets. Weather and temperature conditions greatly affect the business of retail food sales. In fact, the business is so much influenced by weather conditions that it could rightly be called a "weather-related industry."

Nevertheless, one can't conclude that vinyl umbrellas always become strong sellers just because it rains. To begin with, even during the strongest rainstorm it,s impossible to sell vinyl umbrellas unless they're in stock. Umbrella sales also depend on circumstances such as whether rain starts to fall after it has been cloudy since early morning, threatening rain, or whether the rain suddenly came from what was just minutes before a clear blue sky. Even though rain is rain, the customers, degrees of preparedness are different. In the first case, people will have their umbrellas ready, but when the weather has been fair, people will seldom be prepared with their umbrellas.

Note that variables of demand can be compounded too. For instance, when it rains, sales of umbrellas will vary between a store in a residential area and a store in front of a private railroad station located in a suburb. In fact, one variable may have more weight than the other. In this case, the store's situation is of primary importance.

Demand: Varies with Relative Temperature

Just as demand for some items varies considerably depending on whether it's rain or shine, the relative temperature also influences product sales trends to a great degree. I have heard that if the temperature exceeds 30 degrees centigrade (86 degrees Fahrenheit) in summer, sales of soft drinks with high sugar content will stagnate, but carbonated drinks, water and tea will take off. In the case of ice cream, the hot sellers go from ice cream with a high proportion of milkfat to light ice candy and sherbets.

The key demand factor here is a so-called relative temperature, meaning the temperature that the human body perceives. A high of 23 degrees centigrade (73 degrees Fahrenheit) will feel quite hot in

March and April but relatively cool in June or July. Consequently, if such a temperature persists, there will be changes in product sales. Cold soft drinks, for example, will begin to sell well, even in March. On the other hand, during a relatively cool summer when temperatures are lower than usual, warm or even hot foods and drinks may be preferred over cold refreshments. People don't want cold drinks when the weather is like that. If someone feels chilly and goes into a store and finds hot, steaming noodles waiting for them, that's bound to be much more appealing.

The same year that Ito-Yokado suffered it's first loss, some executives and staff members tried to blame it on the cool summer. During the same quarter however, Seven-Eleven increased its sales admirably. Such results demonstrated that what Ito-Yokado's thought was the root of the problem—the cold summer—was not necessarily a good excuse. Instead, it was how the stores responded to it.

Stores and companies that tend to have poor sales during cold summers often fail to respond to the changes in customer psychology or state of mind that the cold summer brings about. They stick to the idea of using summer product lines and sales methods, simply because as the calendar shows it's summer.

7-Eleven stores always try to avoid such fixed ideas by considering the customer's psychology and working from the customer's perspective. As such, they do more to grasp changes in the needs of their customers and respond with products that have tremendous customer appeal.

I've made it a habit to go around and check out several convenience stores when relatively low temperatures continue into the summer months. In the summer of 1998, for example, the temperature continued on the low side for a whole week in the metropolitan Tokyo area. When I went to a 7-Eleven, what did my eyes behold but showcases of Chinese steamed meat buns and buns with bean-jam filling, which are really more like winter foods. Canned hot tea and coffee were sold right next to them. The next day, Japanese noodles were steaming away on the sales floor. And at the other convenience stores? I saw nothing like that. They all had their summer product lines—mostly chilled products. Chilled products for a chilly day.

Seven-Eleven considers the effect that weather and temperature have on sales more seriously than any other retailer. They've even developed a support system that provides weather forecasts to each of the member stores in order to improve the accuracy of the ordering of goods and daily operations. By knowing what to expect, stores can ensure that they are prepared for the demand.

Demand: Varies with Day of Week

The day of the week also affects sales to a certain degree. The sales of lunch items indicate thoroughly different trends on weekdays, when people go to work and children go to school, as compared to Saturdays, Sundays and holidays, when people are at home with their families. Similarly, people tend to spend more money on dinner ingredients during the weekends than they do on weekdays.

In Japan, employees are typically paid once a month, and many receive their pay on the same day. Sales will differ before and after payday. Recognizing how that affects demand, some 7-Eleven stores change their prices for box-lunch lines before and after payday. People may be short on money just before payday and appreciate a slightly lower price. Adjusting prices suits these people's needs, and doing so increases sales and enhances loyalty.

Demand: Varies with Time of Day

As with restaurants, sales at convenience stores and other food stores vary by the clock. For example, 7-Eleven uses a service system wherein box lunches, rice balls, freshly baked breads and other prepared foods are produced and delivered three times a day. These products are always delivered just prior to the peak demand hours, making it possible for the stores to change their lines for breakfast, lunch and dinner. Normally, people will want a breakfast menu in the morning, a lunch menu in the early afternoon and a dinner menu in the evening. Besides particularly energetic young people, not too many people have a good appetite first thing in the morning that they would want to eat the large "Karubi" box lunch. (It is possible, that a line of such large sized box lunches may be in demand from the morning on, however, in stores situated near dorms for single male employees who come home after working the night shift.) Stores can greatly increase their turnover by changing the lineup to satisfy customer needs with different offerings for breakfast, lunch and dinner.

Demand: Varies with Local Events

Along with the demand factors that we've so far discussed, we should also consider the various regional and special events that take place in the markets a store serves.

The following case was actually experienced by a certain cosmetics manufacturer when it set up an experimental store to collect information, which it intended to use for marketing purposes.

Strangely enough, shaving cream especially for armpits sells very well during a certain period in June. When the cosmetics company investigated the reason, they found that the opening of swimming pools in elementary and junior high schools was concentrated around that time. As it turns out, nowadays girls in middle school are precocious and feel they need to shave their armpits before going to the pool. This is one of many examples showing that the sales trends for certain products indeed change in close relation to the special events that take place in our lives.

Seven-Eleven therefore provides each member store with information on calendar event schedules and regional events going on in the vicinity of the store, so that the store managers can make more accurate judgments when ordering goods. While it may not be as dramatic (or traumatic) as a pool opening, things like a scheduled soccer tournament at a nearby school will increase the sales of soda and other cold drinks, for example. Stores also have a way to record their own notes and audio messages about an event in the area that is perhaps only known at the local, store level.

Demand: Varies with Advertising

Of course, in a buyer's market whether or not the manufacturer of an item or the chain selling it runs advertisements on TV or radio also influences sales. Knowing which promotions are airing helps stores proactively respond to the promotional lift.

Seven-Eleven provides sophisticated technology that has made it possible for the people who order goods to view related TV advertisements at the time they order that item.

Demand: Varies with Merchandising

Yet another factor affecting item sales trends is how the store actually sells those items. This includes not only the category assortment itself, but also methods of presentation, such as special sales events, the placement of products in flyers, POP advertisements, in-store demonstrations and so forth.

Additionally, items can be sold differently within a given store. One must also consider where in the store the products are merchandised, in which section of the sales floor they're placed, how they're combined with other products, how the display shelves are arranged, and how the lighting is used. Such factors have a tremendous impact on sales.

Even when vinyl umbrellas are in stock, sales will differ considerably, depending on where they're placed in the store when the rain begins to fall. It depends on whether they're at the back of the store where customers don't notice them, or whether they're at the front of the store, in plain view of all.

Decisions are Made In-Store

It has recently been observed that the way consumers purchase products has changed into the so-called "meeting, contact and discovery" approach. Moreover, it should be pointed out that this trend will become even more pronounced in the future. Reportedly, even when people buy everyday things, they don't know specifically what they will buy until they get into the store.

With the affluence of modern society, we can no longer immediately say what we want when we're asked. The purchase is facilitated and value created when the customer meets, comes into contact with, and discovers information. Many products have great potential to communicate appealing messages but are simply buried on the sales floors because the messages aren't expressed properly.

Most people tend to wait until they come into direct contact with products, product mixes and displays at the storefront to get some idea of what they should cook or eat for dinner. Only then do they decide what to buy. Coming into contact with what they see available in the stores and discovering relevant information pertaining to them facilitates their purchase.

Since this is true even for purchases of daily necessities, it must hold true to a much higher degree for more selective products as in fashion merchandise, entertainment products/services and amenities. It's only natural that even fewer people decide what to buy before they shop for these items. The imagination and creativity that lead to the actual purchase are stimulated when one comes into direct contact with information in a store (or in a catalogue or on the Internet), and their desires take specific shape.

Of course, there's significant influence in the information provided by mass media such as TV, magazines and newspapers before they leave home. But in reality, the information conveyed directly from the storefront has an even greater practical effect in suggesting a new way of life.

Four Ways Information Shapes Demand

The information at the storefront can be divided into the following four categories:

(1) The products themselves

The smell of steaming foods like hot noodles is a good example of something that gets through to people's feelings. If people see steaming foods on a cool day, they'll feel like eating it and warming themselves up. Thus the qualities of the product itself drive demand.

Or a girl might see a stylish sweater in the window and think, "Ah, that's is what I'll wear when I go out with boyfriend next weekend. It'll go well with that skirt and scarf I have, and I'll look really cute and he'll definitely like, and compliment me too." By that point, the sweater ceases to be a mere object. It is now something beyond that, a representation of a way of life that satisfies her desires.

Only products that deliver messages like that and get through to people's feelings can promote a purchase decision. Ordinary goods no longer appeal to people's feelings. The sales trend of an item is determined by the power of the messages it relays to customers, the power to suggest new values in their lives, and the power to stimulate their creativity and imagination.

One must keep this point of view in mind when considering which products to produce and sell. Moreover, the value of those products should be accurately delivered to the point of sale and must be made obvious to the consumer.

(2) The product mix or assortment

Mothers with children who go to schools that don't provide lunches are always looking for nice ideas for their children's lunchboxes. Since they need to prepare lunch every day, they may eventually run out of ideas. Such despair of hopeless repetition is relieved when they go to a supermarket and find a meal solutions section called "Box Lunch Corner" and find a wide assortment of options they can use to make lunch. This is how they meet, come into contact with and discover what they need to know to lead more fulfilling lives. They discover a little bit of wisdom, a new way of preparing a box lunch, and they get excited about the reactions their children will have, and it promotes the purchase of goods sold in this section.

Some messages are communicated by the location of the product in the store. Take the example of a clock for the bathroom. Where should it be placed in the stores in order to attract the attention of customers? Location is the key to maximizing the clock's power to suggest how it can be used. It may not have much appeal if it were placed in the clock section, but if placed in the bathroom products area the possibility of people buying it becomes higher, simply because the location suggests to them how it can be used.

When cross merchandising like this is large in scale, it becomes a type of operation. The convenience store industry is essentially like this. In the convenience store industry, products are selected, gathered, organized and offered together with other service elements under the basic principle of how goods and services should be handled and where they should be offered to satisfy the customer's need for convenience. Some goods and services may be mere bit players in certain types of conventional retail stores, restaurants and service businesses, but when they're assorted under a business concept based on "daily needs for convenience," they stand out as the main characters.

Ready-to-eat foods, magazines and game software, for example, are sold everywhere. When these items are placed with a larger selection of goods grouped with the goal of satisfying the need for convenience, they take on different meanings—and values—than when they're found independently in supermarkets, bookstores and other places. They have a certain profile that communicates their role in satisfying people who seek convenience.

(3) Recommendations and demonstrations

This refers to information dissemination through people. Specifically, the customer will also be much more likely to buy if the store employee engages in suggestive selling. Recently, the term "charismatic sales clerk" has become popular in the Japanese fashion industry, much the way the term "house mannequin" was popular a while ago. The term refers to the employees of stores that sell fashion clothing, particularly those targeting young women. They wear the outfits on the job and coordinate them very smartly. In a subtle way, this communicates certain messages to customers and urges them to buy the products. The cooler the selection, coordination and manner in which the products are worn by the sales clerk, the more persuasive power and charisma she will have. This works much better than the usual display since the message is so much stronger an incentive to buy.

In store demonstrations at department stores and tastings and sampling done in supermarkets and department stores are also effective means of communicating value.

If you are selling juicers, for example, it doesn't help to say, "This is a juicer," and then offer it at a cheap price. It won't be enough. Consumers will likely tell you that they already have one, and that will be the end of it. But if the juicer is presented as an innovative product with great new values, and customers get to taste how good the juice is, even a person who already has a juicer at home is more likely to think, "This is great! I'll replace my old one."

(4) Inventive displays

Inventive displays and presentations are very good at appealing to customers. Conventional display methods, such as gondola end-caps, shelf designs, reserving large surfaces for customer appeal, and other methods work to attract attention to products and the value they provide.

The message that a product projects into people's lives will change dramatically according to how it's conveyed. I believe that communicating product value and suggesting ways in which consumers can use products in their lives will become much more important in the future. The sales trends for the same item will change dramatically in the future according to the way it's sold and how the product value is communicated. Therefore, it will be necessary to examine how things are sold in order to truly understand and track the sales trends for an item.

Chapter 5

The Strategic Use of POS Data for Tanpin Kanri

The tanpin kanri approach to grasping customer demand should not be thought of simply as a technology for merchandise control. Nor is it simply about keeping track of individual product trends. While indeed computers and POS systems make it possible to track each and every item in the store and are powerful tools, tanpin kanri is a strategy that has come about as a necessary consequence of the changes in the times. It a comprehensive approach to grasping demand and centering production, delivery, orders and sales activities around consumer needs.

The real world operational reforms of Ito-Yokado and Seven-Eleven make a good example of the reengineering of methodologies and systems required for tanpin kanri.

As you know, the first step in the process for both companies was to eliminate shelf warmers. How they did that shows the power of tanpin kanri.

To rid itself of slow-moving merchandise, Ito-Yokado didn't just divide merchandise into three categories according to their POS sales volume, A, B and C, and eliminate category C. While this analysis is a conventional control method that may seem superficially in support of the practice of tanpin kanri, it is in fact, fundamentally different. Consider the following:

A cheap, vinyl umbrella is category C merchandise when the weather has been dry for a long time. However, it changes to category A merchandise as soon as the rain begins to fall.

Thus, sales of the same item varies greatly depending on the conditions in which it's sold. It's impossible to determine which items are shelf warmers and which are not, without first considering the factors affecting the market trend of each SKU.

That's why, when Ito-Yokado was about to adopt POS systems and use those for ordering for all its stores, Suzuki voiced his objection. He was against the common notion that POS was a universal solution, saying, "POS isn't a tool for finding products that sell well. Rather, it's a tool for identifying shelf warmers."

While the general acceptance of POS data remains unchanged today, at that time the prevalent understanding in the business world was that POS systems could be used as a means of tracking strong-selling merchandise. To voice a dissenting opinion naturally caused a big stir, and Suzuki had great difficulty getting people to understand.

Ultimately, though, it comes down to a fundamental way of grasping the issue. It's here that the concept of tanpin kanri, as well as the strategy employed in Seven-Eleven's innovative information system for distribution starts to become clear.

Going Beyond POS Data

Generally speaking, people take POS data as information wholesale, without giving it much scrutiny. But is it safe to assume that POS data is the right information to apply at the store, let alone midstream and upstream? Is POS data enough for headquarters product departments to implement production and delivery operations, or for marketing and product development? Can everything—including production by the manufacturer, delivery of merchandise from the wholesaler, and shipping of merchandise from headquarters to retail stores—be driven by POS data?

> *'The business will fall into a depressed state if it uses the POS system to track the sales trends of strong-selling products."*
> *—T. Suzuki*

As already stated, the general understanding is, yes, it's possible to use POS systems to determine which products sell well. In fact, the automatic replenishment systems used by many retailers function this way. At many US retail chains, over half of the product volume is supplied through automatic replenishment. All that is required is to replenish the quantity sold, and the supply process closes the loop. So Suzuki's comments on POS sounded heretical in light of common understanding.

Why can't we use POS as a tool to identify merchandise that sells well? The reason is as follows: The idea of tracking strong-selling merchandise using POS is based on the assumption that one's own store has strong-selling merchandise in the first place. That assumption, however, is the source of the problem.

POS systems can do nothing more than provide past data. Moreover, that data will merely indicate the results of one's own business practices. The data generated by the POS system pertains to trends for the products that one's store already sells, but the system never generates data for goods not handled by that store.

This particular characteristic of POS data can explain the aforementioned view that "the business will fall into a state of equilibrium at a reduced level if it uses the POS system to find strong-selling products." If the store believes strong selling products are to be found among its current offerings, and they rely on the POS system to tell them which those are, their product assortment will stay the same and the store and its sales floor will become dull and unattractive to the customer. But in many cases, performance stagnates and the business fails to maintain its success.

Suzuki believes, and the practice of tanpin kanri recommends, that retailers need to be proactive about new item introductions. What if manufacturers were to believe that, since some of their products are selling well, there's no need to develop and exploit new products? In actuality, though, that's not how they feel, and that's not what they do. Their attitude is that there must be some potential hit product out there that can generate huge demand. Manufacturers are always striving to create something new because they think that what excites the market, creates demand and attracts customers exists among the products that don't exist yet; or at least, not among the products they currently produce and sell. There are countless examples of whole markets being formed by unique, new concepts.

This principle is by no means exclusive to product manufacturing, but applies to retail, as well. The idea that true, strong-selling merchandise exists among the goods and services a business has not yet handled, sold or provided will always motivate the forward progress of that business.

If stores really believed there were strong-selling products that would make a sensation in the market and that these product are not among the goods they currently sell, the store would, in its product development and purchasing operations, strive to bring new items to its shelves. Such measures would ensure that the store, its sales floor and product assortment remain fresh and appealing.

The assumption that good-selling merchandise may exist among the things that haven't yet been created tends to make it difficult to use the approach of tracking the merchandise that already sold, namely POS data. To find something that doesn't exist is where the methodology of "examination, hypothesis and re-examination" comes into play. The existence of potential demand can only be verified through the creation a certain hypothesis, offering it to the market and seeing how it goes.

When one attempts to identify potentially strong-selling products that haven't been handled before, whether it will be accepted will only become clear once you bring the product into the store and test the customer's reaction.

Thus, the true discovery of good-selling merchandise is possible not through looking at POS data, but only through examination, hypothesis and re-examination. If a store believes strong-selling products exist beyond its own sales floor, management needs to operate according to this system and make it a working daily practice.

> 'The POS system is a tool for verifying an action based on a hypothesis." —**T. Suzuki**

This does not, by any means, imply that POS data are irrelevant. If one were to implement the verification by hand, the labor involved would be overwhelming. But POS systems promptly prepare the necessary data for you, indicating part of the trend for each single item. POS data can never provide complete information in the absence of a hypothesis or consideration of other demand factors.

Since that may be a roundabout expression, I'll give an example. Let's assume that 10 units of a certain item were sold yesterday. In an automatic ordering system, the most appropriate order volume is calculated taking into account the present inventory and data from several recent days or weeks, or there may be some complicated mathematical formula for calculating the order.

Even with the application of a sophisticated mathematical model, however, tomorrow refuses easy predictions. The reason 10 units sold last week could be because there were only 10 units in stock. Having that cause-and-effect insight suggests something about the data. What if there were 20 units in stock? Would 18 have sold? It's hard to say that the data showing that 10 units were sold accurately depicts actual market conditions without considering various conditions. The sale of 10 units could be a reflection of the site, the geographical and trade area, competitive conditions, day of the week, whether it was before or after payday, weather and temperature, whether or not there was some special event in the store's vicinity, etc. It would be simple-minded to take action based solely on the POS report showing that 10 units were sold.

More importantly, based on data showing that 10 units were sold in store A, it would be dangerous for headquarters to stock stores B and C with the same products, or for the vendors to decide to deliver them to other stores. Wouldn't it be dangerous for the store to expect yesterday's results tomorrow?

For that to work, the above example relies on the premise that the data generated by the POS system accurately reflects the state of the market. Reality, however, often diverges from theory, and tomorrow's results won't necessarily be logical extensions of past averages. Moreover, it's quite risky to project an image of the past onto tomorrow unless the cause-and-effect relationship is firmly comprehended, meaning you know under what conditions the demand occurred and the results were obtained.

POS data is meaningful only if it's obtained by observing how the product in question was treated in the store. This data would have to include its price, whether or not it was discounted, its display, presentation and shelf arrangement at the store, and its combination with other products. The information to be found there can serve as knowledge that can shape hypothesis about why products sell and what other products might sell too.

Again, the Importance of High Delivery Rates

Prior to the introduction of the POS system, counting stock and placing orders could be considered routine, given that it consisted of hand-counting the number of products sold and reporting that figure in accordance with a prescribed procedure. An even simpler yet more "advanced" method of replenishment was to maintain a minimum stock volume previously determined for each item. Almost no judgment is required from the store personnel, so order placement of this kind is also routine.

It was already troublesome to conduct an inventory check at the end of each month. But if this needed to be done once a week or a couple of times a week or even every day for some items, retailers would certainly face an immense amount of labor. In that respect, POS is a wonderful tool, and there can be little doubt that stock checking has become the chief application of it (other than checkout, of course). But the problem is that tracking stock via POS isn't accurate unless the receipt status of goods is accurately checked as well.

From a data-processing perspective, the most convenient method of checking the stock status is to correlate order data and POS data. The amount ordered minus the amount sold is the stock on hand. A certain contrivance is required, however, to check the status of stock using POS. POS data shows the sales trend but doesn't realistically show the status of accumulated stock remaining on the sales floor. At a delivery rate of about 50 percent, for example, as was seen at Ito-Yokado prior to the implementation of its operational reforms, more than 40 percent of the goods ordered would not make it to stores due to failed delivery, delayed delivery or out-of-stock. Under such low delivery rate conditions, it's impossible to track stock by subtracting POS data from order data. More work would be required in order to obtain data on goods actually delivered, based on invoices, receiving slips and to correlate that with POS data. Thus delivery rate comes into focus for the timely checking of stock status. This is critical to the management process of tanpin kanri.

Seven-Eleven has set a high delivery rate standard which ranges from 99 to nearly 100 percent as a prerequisite for the accurate determination of stock status.

Hypothesis and Verification

To begin with, shelves need to be cleared of shelf warmers. Even if new merchandise can be placed on the sales floor together with the weaker merchandise, the possible added value of the new merchandise is buried among the shelf warmers and the possibility that the customer will recognize the value of the new products is lost.

POS is an effective tool for locating shelf warmers. In that sense the ultimate exploitation of POS is as a tool to find shelf warmers indeed helps cultivate strong-selling merchandise. In order for the retailer to fill the store and sales floor with good-selling merchandise, it's necessary to bring new goods that one hasn't handled before into the store, and this is done on a certain hypothesis which is verified through POS data.

Good selling merchandise is found through cultivation. By continually bringing in new merchandise based on the development and verification of new hypotheses, retailers can leverage POS to identify the merchandise that sells well.

Seven-Eleven was first company in the Japanese distribution industry to introduce POS terminals in large numbers and had this function. The function of the terminal was limited to the tracking of single-item trends and did not incorporate the other more costly functions that were commercially available at that time.

Order Accuracy

As previously discussed, low ordering accuracy has a decidedly negative effect on the commerce and management of a store. Low order accuracy, such as an order in excess of actual demand, results in dead stock and undermines profit. At the same time, it renders the sales floor and product assortments unattractive to customers. The point of examining the sales situation, forming a hypothesis and then checking the results is to create better accuracy.

It's worse when you consider that orders placed by retailers at a low degree of accuracy will eventually bounce back as returned goods. This is particularly true when the retailer holds a strong position in the business relationship. The vendor has no choice but to accept the returns.

Consider the example of a store that orders a certain brand of cigarettes from a dealer as an out-of-stock of this product becomes imminent. If, however, the dealer has no stock or the delivery will likely be too late, the store brings in an alternative item that falls within the same product category. Faced with bare shelves, the dealer has no choice but to deliver alternative items to make up for the scarcity. While such tactics worked in the seller's market, it's no longer wise in a buyer's market, where customers have become more selective. A departure from the seller's market would lead instead to team merchandising and the mutual exchange of information and supplier and retailer would ward against failed or delayed deliveries and out-of-stocks..

Out-of-stocks on hit products are more likely to occur because commercial popularity often tends to be concentrated on a single product. Yet, when a certain item is selling very well, deliveries in response to sudden additional orders are likely to be late. Replenishment needs can't be met unless the trading partners established a team system, and that team works together toward productive "engagement" rather than mere "negotiation." Unless they do so, manufacturers cannot adequately produce the appropriate quantities, nor can retailers expect timely product delivery, no matter how well they've sold in the past.

Accordingly, the information strategy for the distribution industry has to begin with the issue of ordering accuracy. Tanpin kanri helps the retailer not only improve order accuracy, but provide better information upstream.

Orders of low accuracy also have a negative effect on product vendors since simply don't provide a true picture of the market, say if an order is placed for poor-selling products or if no order is placed for strong-selling ones. Implementing production and delivery against such inaccurate information runs the risk that the organization will diverge from the true state of the market. Since losses are born from inaccuracy in ordering, it's an indication that the placement of orders is not a routine activity. Nor should it be subject to cost cutting or labor-saving measures. Instead, it should be an important management process that is absolutely critical to the survival of the business.

Retail orders placed with a high degree of accuracy can serve as very useful marketing information for manufacturers and vendors.

One of the tenets of tanpin kanri is that those who make products and distribute them should take into account what useful information the retail field, or downstream, has to offer in terms of marketing, production and even logistics. So should product departments and buyers at the retail headquarters learn from stores. But POS systems still haven't been fully utilized as tools for marketing. Other tools are needed to adequately provide effective marketing information for the entire demand chain, and tanpin kanri technology is it.

Sharing Information to Benefit Production, Delivery and Sales

Information flow in supply chain management always heads in a single direction. POS data flows back toward the midstream and upstream.

Traditional industrial systems have a similar dynamic, in that there's only an arterial flow, i.e., a constant flow from upstream to downstream. No venous flows exist. Just as such an industrial system can't achieve the true rationalization of production operations, information systems based on the back-flow of POS data in a single direction from downstream cannot truly rationalize production and delivery operations, either.

An information system for demand chain management, like Seven-Eleven's, is different from that found in supply chain management because it's bi-directional. Information doesn't simply flow back from the retail sales field; information from upstream and midstream flow downstream. As we'll see in the next chapterl, that's pivotal to the whole effort.

There's a fundamental point here. Historically production, warehousing and sales were integrated operations. Bread used to be sold in the same place it was produced, and customers had to go there to buy bread. But where products were made and where they were sold gradually separated as modern industrialization transformed traditional business into one that pursued scale through concentrated production and warehousing and the proliferation of sales venues.

The disintegration that came from that resulted in various inconveniences that never before existed. As people began to expect greater satisfaction and consumers became more critical in terms of value selection, the negative aspects of disintegration began cropping up in the value-determination process.

The Discrepancies of Disintegration

Where the manufacturing and warehousing operations are separate from the sales location, there are four major troublesome aspects of discrepancy.

(1) Discrepancy in time
(2) Discrepancy in space (distance)
(3) Discrepancy in one's senses
(4) Discrepancy in feelings

Discrepancy 1 refers to a gap in time and the timing between actual demand and the production or stocking operation. Deteriorating freshness is a serious problem caused by this gap.

As is the case with 1, the importance of innovation in information and logistics can be traced back to 2, the discrepancy in space (distance). How can we overcome the gap in time and space between production and sales operations, or from warehouses and distribution centers to stores. Trading partners that take measures to shorten these gaps stand to be winners, especially as customers become more demanding.

The essence of system innovation is the attempt to narrow these gaps as much as possible thus retaining the benefits and economy of scale of a concentrated production and warehousing operation.

This is where the basis of the Ito-Yokado Group's corporate reforms, as well as the basis of Seven-Eleven's innovation in information systems and logistics. The goal is a team merchandising system that combines production, delivery and sales operations and demand chain management.

Discrepancies in sense and feeling (3 and 4) can also be overcome to a considerable degree by innovation in information and communication systems. This is because the frustration felt by the production or delivery field, which believes it isn't correctly informed of consumers' needs and changes thereof, is the cause of various problems that exist between the supply and demand sides.

As retail customers becoming more and more strict in their selections of value, this discrepancy in feelings will emerge as a big problem that could come as a real shock to the industrial system. As earlier examples have shown, product lifecycles are becoming ever shorter and the concentration of strong-selling products is becoming more extreme. Sales trends for the same items differ to a great degree, according to geographical area, trade area, competitive conditions, customer group, the site and type of operation. Moreover, sales differ greatly even between stores belonging to the same chain. It depends on the situation at each store, the day of the week, the temperature, weather, and even the time of day. If manufacturers and wholesalers can't get a handle on these various factors, there's bound to be discrepancy in feelings.

An information system is expected to overcome this communication gap that exists between manufacturers, wholesalers and retailers. Ito-Yokado, for example, had tried to get rid of shelf warmers at the beginning of its operational reforms. But bitter complaints were heard from vendors. Their argument was the following: "We product marketers make huge investments toward bringing a single product to market, and some products need time to be accepted. If they're kicked off the sales floor for poor sales too early, even potentially strong-selling products might be deprived of the chance and the marketer would suffer significant losses."

Of course, no marketer will produce a product if they think it won't sell well. They must put forth their own marketing effort, conduct research-and-development operations, and put the products on the market with a great sense of purpose and passion. But if their best intentions don't properly reach the people in the sales field, the following questions arise. Depending on how these questions are answered, the treatment of the products in stores might be completely different.

- Why are such products developed and produced?
- What sense of meaning are they given?
- How do they differ from those already put on the market?
- What are their advantages, as compared to similar products?
- What should be done to properly convey to the consumer the purposes and intentions of the manufacturer?
- Can retailers sympathize with the developers, manufacturers and suppliers of products as if they themselves had done the job?

By sharing in the information about products, retailers begin to have intentions and passions of their own about them. Then, even if a product doesn't sell immediately, the retailer might be able to make customers understand its potential value. They'll also refrain from the practice of quickly delisting products that don't sell well right away. The retailer will start to nurture them and take the time to sell them, thereby erasing the discrepancy in feelings about the product between the manufacturer and the store. The purposes, intentions and passions of the people who engaged in the production or supply of the product have to be conveyed, in the form of information, to the point of sale.

Communication and information systems convey that purposeful and intentional information from upstream or midstream to the downstream channel and back are the machines of tanpin kanri.

"Buyers shouldn't negotiate business with salespeople and wholesalers."   **—T. Suzuki**

Traditionally, negotiations between retailers and vendors were mostly concerned with deal conditions. But information necessary to a proper understanding of the product—including the purposes and intention of its production—was rarely the subject of discussion. There were few opportunities for salespeople to convey to customers the purposes and intentions concerning the production and its development. There was little chance of furthering their understanding. To some extent, buyers lacked a sense of purpose.

US consumer product marketers, wholesalers and retailers now employ the process of category management for such purposes, although the investigation is less granular than with tanpin kanri. Working with retailers to communicate the "why" of a product as much as the "what," puts the focus on product attributes and ends some value-defeating trade practices of the past.

Under the prevailing circumstances there was no communication with the actual sales environment. That's why Seven-Eleven and Ito-Yokado required their buyers to obtain appropriate product information by tracking down the reasons for a product's development rather than becoming absorbed in discussions over deal conditions with salespeople. In short, we've seen a shift from "negotiation" to "collaboration."

Suzuki asserted that the buyers themselves should also work with purpose and intention, if necessary all the way through to the implementation of joint product development and test marketing.

A greater depth of communication between the maker's or wholesaler's side and the seller's side enables the seller to form a more sophisticated view regarding the practice of examination, hypothesis and re-examination. Through orders, product assortment and sales operations, which are implemented with purpose and intentions or through the application of a hypothesis, verification will have more effect and true accuracy of ordering will be achieved.

These orders will flow back to midstream and upstream via another information system, eventually leading the way in production and delivery operations. If only POS data flowed back, it would be hard to conduct production and delivery operations based on actual market demand.

Accurate orders placed through the retailer's field operation will bring production and delivery operations that are much closer to actual market demand. To do that, the establishment of yet another information system is absolutely essential, one that can send a constant flow of information and communication from the upstream and midstream to the downstream. Such information will eventually serve as a powerful tool for those in the sales field who engage in the practice of listening, thinking and learning, or in other words the process of examination, hypothesis and re-examination.

A notable feature of the tanpin kanri technology is that it has in itself an advanced system of information transmission and communication directed to those in the sales field through various media, making it much more than the mere automation of computerized communications.

Chapter 6

The Human Factor: Beyond Supply Chain Management

C hanging times demand innovative ways of thinking.

"Labor and time should be spent on order placement."
—T. Suzuki

The reason that Suzuki stresses accuracy in ordering is a fundamental understanding of the business isn't predicated on commodities. While certainly demand for commodities does exist in some channels, customers have become selective and sophisticated in the buyer's market. Value-added products are at the center of demand. Since value is price-driven, it's served by economy of scale.

For all but the largest retailers, commodity business can be risky. Not only is it low-margin, but there's a higher risk of monopolization in such an environment, where only a limited number of players can survive. International competition is also unavoidable.

If I were asked whether tanpin kanri is necessary for all product genres today, I would reply with a definitive "no." Even today, tanpin kanri is not necessary in a commodity or discount type of operation.

Although there are various interpretations as to what a commodity is, I define it as something that is purchased on the basis of its demand as being of a certain product category. It's something consumers demand mainly because of its functional value, instead of more critically on the basis of their own sense of value. With commodities, products are interchangeable, so out-of-stocks cease to be a major issue since the danger of getting stuck with unsalable merchandise is slim. Customers are not selective so as long as the function is served and will typically buy up commodities if prices are reduced.

Accuracy of ordering is less of an issue since product lifecycles are not shortened. Further, it's unnecessary to conduct a thorough verification of the trends of individual commodities and how their surroundings and other demand factors affect them. Nor is it necessary to devise a marketing strategy by drawing a hypothesis from such examination.

The placement of orders for so-called "regular" products—meaning products in which one deals continuously—is conducted on the basis of replenishing these items because the product sold well. In that context, there's no room for human interpretation since the number of products to be replenished is to exactly match the number sold.

Further, only rough preparation of the sales environment is needed for commodities. That means retailers need only set up a big sales space so that it can be easily approached by the customer, and then line up a large number of products and advertise the price. There's no value produced downstream in this environment. Time and effort shouldn't be expended, and that includes order placement. It's a non-value-added cost requiring neither tanpin kanri nor the pursuit of accuracy in ordering.

Tanpin kanri is different from many so-called demand chain approaches because, rather than looking at ordering as merely a routine activity, it leverages it into an opportunity to add value.

Many retailers look to make ordering as unattended as possible or entrust it entirely to others through auto-replenishment or vendor-managed inventory (VMI) programs. This is done because the ideal of supply chain management is to minimize the costs, labor and time required to complete such a routine tasks, or in order to shift internal costs to external ones. Indeed many people feel vendors who place orders on their behalf are good service providers.

The very idea of ECR and supply chain management. Indeed, these have created a sensation in the Japanese business world. Moreover, the arrival of ECR and supply chain management in Japan was very much in keeping with its technological concept and system development, in place since the introduction of the first POS system.

"We don't place an order because a product has sold well, we place the order because we believe the product will sell well."

*—**T. Suzuki***

The philosophy of Seven-Eleven—in fact, the entire Ito-Yokado Group—with respect to order placement is condensed in the above statement. "Believe the product will sell well" implies that there is some subjective judgment on the part of the person ordering—some feeling they have. Indeed, orders are placed on the basis of a hypothesis and as such, cannot be automated. This subjective order placement based on hypothesis cannot be routine.

Ordering requires thought and hypothesis. That's why Seven-Eleven and Ito-Yokado invest as much effort, labor and time in the process of order placement.

This is key to the information system at Seven-Eleven and Ito-Yokado and their success in the market.

It is these Japanese companies, Seven-Eleven and Ito-Yokado, that created a trend that was diametrically opposed to the mainstream of the industry. The recognition that times had changed—from a seller's market to a buyer's market—would necessitate wide-ranging shifts in perception, from the method of POS system utilization to the content of information system for distribution, the direction of innovation in logistics systems as well as production distribution, and chain operation and structure itself.

Supply chain management has been actively discussed in the distribution industry and among manufacturers themselves. It refers to a system of POS data utilization to enhance efficiency in product supply and delivery. This method implies that product supply is conducted according to the sales trends obtained from the POS system. Supply chain management is based on the view of replenishment that says "as they're sold, resupply them."

Indeed, with supply chain management, the whole procedure is supposed to proceed very rationally: A retailer's storefront is networked with wholesalers and manufacturers and POS data goes through this network. Ultimately products in the right quantity (that is, the quantity sold) are sent to the right location. This system makes it possible to achieve labor savings in order placement, which isn't supposed to generate value. People in charge of order placement don't have to be in the store. The POS and computer systems can serve as useful tools for the rationalized of distribution of product. As wholesalers and manufacturers are able to implement production and delivery operations that match market demand, one can achieve a loss-free business led by the downstream initiative.

Supply chain management appears to be a rational method well suited to the times, but that's a superficial understanding of the system. Basically, it's a system built on the past—staying well within the concept of commodities—and as such, regards products in that light.

The premise is that POS data truly conveys the state of the market, as well as the changes taking place in that market.

What is required is to realize that production, delivery, product assortment and sales activities that correspond to actual market demand can be possible only when they're based on a certain system. That is, a system in which the personnel in each store interpret data through the operational cycle of hypothesis and verification. Subsequently, production and delivery operations are directed by the order placement of these front-line people. This is the basis of the "demand chain management" concept as applied by Seven-Eleven and Ito-Yokado.

Which is more accurate—order placement by supply chain management, which is ideally unattended and as automated as possible, or order placement by demand chain management, which is implemented on the basis of the initiative and direction of each store? Which has a closer relationship to market demand? The answer should already be clear. Naturally, production and delivery operations led by such order placement more closely match the needs of the market.

What is the fundamental difference between supply chain management and demand-chain management in terms of the system application? Supply chain management is doubtless a revolutionary innovation by comparison to the tired old practices it replaced.

Certainly they're similar, but they remain distinct from one another. Supply chain management is a continuation of the idea based on the upstream and midstream, in which it's up to the wholesalers and manufacturers to determine production and shipment based on the POS data returned from the sales field downstream. After all, as the name suggests, supply chain management is a system for suppliers that pursues efficiency for them through the use of computers and communication systems.

Supply chain management is predicated on the understanding that the data on single-product trends collected by the POS system reflects the actual market. Another major feature of this system is, as it is with the traditional idea of "product out/market in," that the role of the retailer (sales field) remains out of consideration, especially with regard to production, delivery and shipment operations. To put it simply, daily order placement by the retailer (excluding negotiations concerning inventory and order placement between the sales field at the storefront and the product department at headquarters) is not considered significant. That way, the ideal form of rationalization for supply chain management is the maximum automation of order-placement operations.

The fundamental defect of supply chain management, however, lies in the fact that POS data doesn't necessarily reflect the actual state of the market. Moreover, supply chain management can't create an effective touchpoint for customer relationship management, which currently has emerged as a major theme in the business world. In short, this system will ultimately reach a dead end, void of potential.

Human Action: Key Factor in the Information Process

Given the assumption that value is generated in the consumer's mind, what naturally gains importance is the presence of humans in the field, that is, in the place where people and products encounter each other and values are determined. How deeply can one be involved in the process of value formation, where values are generated in the consumer's mind? It's in one's involvement in this process that information on market demand is generated, thereby guiding enterprise business operations, including production, delivery and sales.

Humans play a main role in the information process. This is expressed excellently in the vision of C&C (Computers and Communication) at Japanese system vendor NEC Corp., which says, "Computers, including POS systems, are servants to humans." As this expression suggests, the data generated by the POS system is a tool with which humans can acquire more advanced knowledge.

Again, however, it isn't possible to grasp market demand via the POS system alone, because values can't be grasped as easily as was possible for commodities. Just knowing how many sold doesn't reflect demand from the market.

Value formation lies in the practice of examination, hypothesis and re-examination by personnel in the field. Here I'll cite the Buddhist phrase "Listening, thinking and learning." This has much the same meaning as the scientific methodology of examination, hypothesis and re-examination, but it's somewhat more to the point in terms of the bi-directional or interactive relationship that has lately become the dominant concept. In this environment of "listening, thinking and learning," which is the basis of the information process itself, we humans are the subject.

The nature of demand chain management that Seven-Eleven has been so consistently pursuing is based on the belief that humans play the primary role in information processing. This is the fundamental difference between tanpin kanri and supply chain management, the ideal of which is maximally unattended operation and automation of the supply chain.

Verifying Cause and Effect Relationships

POS data showing the sales quantity of a SKU can be transformed into information by verifying the relationship between cause and effect. That process is best implemented by the person who takes action based on his or her own hypothesis. One cannot effectively evaluate the result of an action without the benefit of personally knowing the hypothesis upon which the action was taken.

POS data can't generate knowledge by itself. However, when you study the cause and effect, that data is transformed into information, and information applied becomes knowledge. Therefore the process of verification is most effective when it's conducted by the person who took action based on their own hypothesis.

Logically, the role of placing orders should be given to those who are engaged in sales activities on the sales floor. With this as a pivotal measure, we would obtain the greatest benefit from a system that boldly entrusts the entire process to the subjective view of the staff, be it decisions on the product line, shelf arrangement or sales method.

Chapter 7

Pioneering Tanpin Kanri Technology at Seven-Eleven

The advanced information system that Seven-Eleven Japan now boasts is unparalleled in the world. Over the 20-odd years of the company's ongoing customer-oriented business revolution, it has spent some 200 billion yen ($1.7 billion) on information technology—a remarkable record of investment, by any measure.

The foundation for the system was largely shaped by the early operational and distribution challenges that surrounded 7-Eleven stores in Japan. Namely, every store had to carry a wide variety of merchandise, small stores quickly went out-of-stock on popular items and the economics of frequent deliveries weren't favorable for stores and vendors alike.

These conditions put pressure on Seven-Eleven to hone its accuracy in ordering. It took a major investment to grow in an environment where demand varied from store to store, requiring the company to be in step with the individual, specific needs of every market, even as it is constantly changing.

Humble Beginnings

The ordering system at Seven-Eleven began as an extremely primitive one, not unlike what was being used by other chain stores at the time. Each store placed telephone orders with each of its wholesalers from an order book in which suppliers and their items were listed. This method worked well when there were just one or two stores, but when the number increased to dozens the vendors and wholesalers began to complain. Answering the calls from all of the stores by itself was a lot of work.

Ordering this way was labor intensive for the store side, as well. So the first efficiency implemented by Seven-Eleven addressed this issue through the introduction of a "slip" system. To begin with, the slip system changed the entry sequence in the order book from the previous wholesaler-based sequence to one based on how products were physically displayed on the gondolas. Rather than looking all over the store for a single supplier's products, the person ordering could now easily see where each item was located. This saved considerable time and effort.

The slip system also eliminated the need for each member store to call wholesalers directly. The pages in the order book had perforated tabs, and once the required order quantities were filled in, all the person ordering had to do was tear out the tab and hand it to an order-slip collection agent from the district office when that person visited the store.

The collected order slips were then transmitted electronically via telephone line from the district office to a computer at headquarters. The computer then sorted the store orders compiling order summaries by vendor, which were subsequently picked up by the vendors. This too was a dramatic improvement in efficiency.

It's interesting to note that the stores had a tendency to order more than what they needed when placing orders over the phone, perhaps due to a sense of guilt associated with placing small orders, or vanity.

Be that as it may, since the new system put the person ordering on the sales floor, it enabled the stores to place orders that more closely reflected actual demand, helping reduce the occurrence of overstocks. Prior to that time, the stores had many things to do when placing orders, so they didn't have time to study merchandise and sales trends. The new system gave the stores extra time, which they could use for making better forecasts. This was the start of the tanpin kanri practice and was important to the development of Seven-Eleven's business.

Unlike the traditional order system, which was based on phone calls from a store to a wholesaler, the new system generated a slip that recorded the store's order. This order record served to streamline receiving and also enabled the member store to better evaluate each vendor's delivery rates.

The new system brought significant benefits to vendors too. They no longer had to receive separate orders from individual stores over the phone, compile them, and create purchase slips. They required less manpower, and naturally, errors dropped substantially.

Terminal 7 (1978)

The next step, in July of 1978, was the introduction of "Terminal 7" at all of the 450 member stores, a computer-based, online order-entry system.

This system was still a very primitive one given the technological capabilities of the systems Seven-Eleven now employs. Terminal 7 used an order book in which items were entered according to the display sequence on the gondolas, as with the slip system. This time, each item listed in the order book was assigned a bar code. The person ordering would take this order book to the sales floor, check the merchandise on the gondola and then scan the bar code for each item and an appropriate quantity code using a light pen. The scanned data was recorded in the Terminal 7 unit which was leased to each store—a proprietary technology developed by Seven-Eleven—and then transmitted to a host computer in Ohio via communications satellite.

Once at the host computer, order data was sorted by vendor and transmitted online to the respective vendors' distribution centers where the actual picking and shipping of merchandise took place. Each vendor also leased the proprietary Seven-Eleven terminal for a nominal fee.)

At the time, Terminal 7 drew the attention of the international distribution community, being that it was the first order system to use online links via satellite. It was just the company's first step toward the use of information technology as a powerful weapon. It had more to do to enhance the accuracy of ordering and revitalize Seven-Eleven's member stores with the flow of information.

Seven-Eleven had by this time adopted different order cycles for different categories of merchandise. The company was using six order books for as many order cycles and was sending updates to the order books every four weeks in order to keep pace with new items and changing market conditions. The order books were continually revised, and new editions were delivered to each store twice a year. Although their content was rudimentary, the order books also contained helpful information that the member stores could use to better understand merchandise assortments and place more accurate orders.

So even at that early date, Seven-Eleven had been sharing product information from the headquarters' Product Department with member stores. One such source was a Merchandise Catalogue, which included an assortment of full-color photos and other pertinent information about products. The catalogue was sent to each store once a week, indicating the frequency with which the company was introducing and recommending new items. This rapid pace mirrored the shortened lifecycles to which products were subject and the rush toward product development among manufacturers.

The merchandise catalogue introduced as many as 80 to 90 items per week, together with nearly 60 pages of information describing them. This information included not only the basics of name, content, supplier and cost, but it also contained information regarding the optimal positioning of each item in the context of current consumer demand, the store's location and the customer groups that were most likely to benefit from the item. There were even tips on how to sell it.

The merchandise catalog helped member stores respond dynamically to fast-changing market conditions by cutting out slow moving items, replacing them with new, potentially hot-selling ones. It was a way for stores to keep the merchandise mix looking fresh in the eyes of the customer.

Individual stores played an active role in deciding their own merchandise mixes. From the recommended list of items selected by the Product Department at headquarters, a store could choose those items that best met the needs of its customers, based on the store's first-hand assessment and familiarity with its specific neighborhood. Letting the store choose items meant that the store had to have the information about each item included on the merchandise list. Optimal information makes for the optimal selection of merchandise, the optimal sales method for each item and the optimal order.

As Seven-Eleven grew larger, however, a new system would be needed. Once the network of stores exceeded 2,000, the order-book system became too expensive. The paper and printing costs associated with updates and revisions were simply too great, and the manpower required was enormous.

Building Logistical Efficiency

Online order placement is now commonplace among suppliers, distributors and retailers, but in those days it was a masterful innovation in efficiency. The system significantly improved operation on the vendor's side too. Unlike the slip system that preceded it, the online ordering system eliminated the need for the vendor to make a trip to headquarters simply to pick up the order slips. Neither was it necessary to process the slips and forward delivery instructions to the distribution center. It was automatic and the savings in time, money and effort were dramatic.

The new system brought remarkable efficiency chiefly in three areas. First, an order slip, delivery slip and accounting slip were generated as a set for each transaction between the vendor and the 7-Eleven store. Secondly, information required for the picking of merchandise at the distribution center—including how many cases of which items must be delivered to which store, or how much in the way of new supplies must be sent from the vendor's headquarters to the distribution center—was automatically sent to the vendor's terminal. Thirdly, the output included a delivery list (which also served as instructions for loading the truck) specifying which items were to be delivered in what quantities to each of the 7-Eleven stores along the route. The whole process was seamless from start to finish.

The data on accounts receivable from each store was automatically stored in the computer terminal, so that at the end of the month, the vendor could simply bring the data to headquarters on a floppy disk. Gone were the days when vendors had to spend their time generating an invoice for each delivery made to a store. This system represented the early stages in the creation of the advanced logistics system that Seven-Eleven uses today.

Developing systems with benefits for trading partners as well became a key factor in Seven-Eleven's ongoing business innovations. The fundamental idea was "we rise and you rise, too."

Reducing Lead Time from Order to Delivery

The new system produced tremendous advantages at the store, headquarters and vendor levels. Overall, it meant a reduction in lead-time from order to delivery. Indeed, the delivery lead-time was reduced by a whole day from what it had been under the old system.

The longer it takes from the placement of an order to the delivery of that order, the more stock a store must keep as a means of preventing out-of-stocks. With the longer lead-times imposed by Seven-Eleven's planned order-delivery schedule and limited space, the store is forced to balance, on one hand, living at constant risk of bad inventory—shelf warmers—while on the other hand, fearing that it's stock of fast-selling items might run out. Shorter lead-times are needed to give a store the flexibility to keep up with changes in the market, preventing out-of-stocks while at the same time, keeping stock keeping requirements at the store to a minimum. Shorter delivery times are important to tanpin kanri since they help the store "procure optimal items in optimal quantities at optimal timing under optimal conditions," one of Seven-Eleven's goals.

In practice, certain items such as box lunches and other perishable goods are delivered to 7-Eleven stores three times daily. This was made possible by a series of efforts in reengineering aimed at reducing the lead-times required. When Seven-Eleven introduced the Terminal 7 system, it began the task of creating an environment in which "market fitness" (the appropriateness and adaptability of merchandise) could be improved with attention to merchandise mixes at individual stores.

The First Generation Total Information System (1982)

While they're commonplace today, few people may realize that the current prevalence of electronic ordering systems was partly inspired by Seven-Eleven. As far back as 1982, the company had a groundbreaking mechanism for ordering, which featured a handheld terminal called an EOB (electronic order book). The EOB combined with the POS system composed the new "Total Information System," and was just the first in a series of systems that Seven-Eleven developed for order processing.

Orders for each item were sent from the store to the vendor using a handy electronic order terminal, which connected to the store's networked computer. This made it possible to automatically check the stock status at each store for each item by subtracting the POS-recorded sales quantity from the quantity entered in the computer.

Embracing Change

When the company first decided to develop an EOB system, Suzuki ordered the project leader to develop it in six months. However, computer manufacturers all refused to accept Seven-Eleven's request, claiming such development would take at least three years. But Suzuki refused to give in. He ordered the project leader to try again, saying, "Nothing is impossible in this day and age when man can set foot on the moon." Refusing to wait three years, Suzuki insisted on finishing the project in six months. He was operating according to the fundamental business principle of "responding to change." Even at that time, three years meant the possibility of great and unforeseen change. The world was shifting gears at ultra-high speed, and technology was moving forward rapidly. Suzuki wanted to respond quickly.

The needs were immediate. The 7-Eleven franchise was expanding at a remarkable rate. Even the best system design at the time might become obsolete given the three years needed to develop it. Furthermore, a system design that was fine for the current 2,000 stores might not work with a network of 3,000 stores. Rather than looking at things based on past experience, the idea was to anticipate the emergence of unexpected issues down the path of progress. From that point on, Seven-Eleven continually upgraded its systems, much the way a crab will cast off its shell for a new one—in response to changes and to meet the needs of member stores.

To accommodate the EOB, a Terminal Controller unit was leased to member stores in place of the Terminal 7 units. Under the Terminal 7 system, order placement remained dependent on order books. The person ordering had to bring the order books right out onto the sales floor in order to make entries. The new system made physical order books completely unnecessary. The new Terminal Controller with a built-in floppy-disk drive was an original solution developed by Seven-Eleven as a way to combine computer-terminal and memory—storage functions in one unit. Since it was only the size of a suitcase, the Terminal Controller could easily be installed in a store's back office.

The handheld EOB terminal was a compact device that an employee could operate with one hand. The user would connect the EOB device to the Terminal Controller in the back office to download necessary information from the master file of items carried at the store. A variety of information could be displayed on the handheld's LCD screen, some of which was impossible to obtain under the previous system of static order books. Certainly, this depth of information became a powerful tool for decision making in the day-to-day ordering process.

Information Displayed on the EOB
- Item name
- Selling price
- Gross margin rate
- The specified day of the week for delivery
- Delivery once a day or twice a day
- Order unit
- Minimum order quantity
- Item priority

- Pre-determined minimum stock quantity of the item at a particular store
- Key instructions that must be referenced when ordering an item, such as the delivery period and selling period from the date of manufacture (expiration date)
- Information necessary for accuracy in ordering, such as the weighting of the order on a particular date, such as a holiday
- Past order/sales results

Items were still displayed according to the planogram of the particular gondola. So, the person ordering simply moved down the gondola while referring to the information for each item displayed on the LCD screen. He or she considered the information presented and input the order quantity for the item into the EOB terminal using its keypad.

After completing the order entry for a single merchandise category, the person would connect the EOB to the Terminal Controller to upload the order data to it. From there, the data would be sent online to the host computer. When the first category was finished, the user could download the order book for the next merchandise category, return to the sales floor and repeat the process. This encouraged the person ordering to consider products category-by-category, the step-by-step approach was actually due to limitations in memory capacity at the time.

Each incoming order was checked against the master files of respective stores, master files of vendors, and master files of all items registered in the 7-Eleven network. Sorted orders were then output to the vendors' terminals.

This new system not only dramatically improved operational efficiency in and among headquarters, stores and vendors, it also marked the start of Seven-Eleven's full-fledged commitment to the strategic use of information technology.

The EOB opened up the possibility for store-by-store merchandise planning, which would enable each of the 7-Eleven stores to tailor itself to the conditions of its local market. Floppy disks inserted in each store's Terminal Controller contained electronic order books representing specific merchandise carried by that store. Therefore, the master files were different at all 2,000 stores. Each maintained its own master files for creating store-specific assortments. Accordingly, it became much more of a reality for each store to place orders and/or maintain a merchandise assortment reflecting the needs of its customers. It was a dynamic system with which individual stores could quickly and easily respond to what happened in their environment.

Earlier system innovations at Seven-Eleven had emphasized rationalization in the ordering process, but they had yet to touch on improving quality in ordering or ordering accuracy. With the introduction of its next system, however, the company would turn its focus to helping individual stores to reflect market conditions in a more timely manner so that each could ensure an optimal mix of merchandise with a high degree of market fitness.

The software of the new system's terminals incorporated approximately 30 different utilities. This software offered higher level benefits in areas such as operations, distribution and administration.

At the time, Seven-Eleven believed that efficiency in work processes was secondary, and instead focused on building a database of marketing information. This was done with the assumption that if marketing could be done more effectively, the logical result would be an enhancement in productivity. It believed that the realization of market value should come first and that corporate efficiency would follow.

Given that the market was changing rapidly and product lifecycles were becoming shorter, stores that carried a fixed assortment couldn't keep pace. Even under the earlier Terminal 7 system headquarters had been busy frequently updating the items registered in the order book and periodically revising it to ensure flexibility.

It became essential, even for individual stores operating under the same franchise, to ensure a mix that was optimized to the store's own market conditions. To do so, they had to understand how demand varied for an item depending on the trade area, site, customer group, competitive circumstances and so on.

The introduction of the POS system, followed by the EOB and Terminal Controller system, were but a prelude to Seven-Eleven's full-scale use of information technology.

In September of 1982, actually several months before the launch of the EOB system, the company began the multistage introduction of its POS system. Their technological savvy is noteworthy-Seven-Eleven Japan wa the first chain store to simultaneously introduce POS across its entire franchise network. The point was to collect point-of-purchase data which would indicate the sales trends for each item.

The system also captured customer-group data under four categories: children, students, housewives and others. The POS register was constructed so that the cashbox wouldn't open unless a customer category key was pressed for each transaction. The customer group, a POS time stamp and data on each item sold could be stored on a floppy disk through the Terminal Controller. It goes without saying that this database furnished each member store with valuable information.

For example, it revealed how customer groups changed in different time slots at each store, and how those changes affects the movement of specific items. This is powerful information in retail marketing. It can be used for determining what orders should be placed, what the merchandise mix should be, how the products should be merchandised, and even how a store should schedule its employee labor.

Of the POS data recorded in the master files of each store, non-urgent data was collected once a week and input to the host computer for processing. The company saw no urgency in checking data daily for all items and felt that such an effort would cost too much in relation to its return. Seven-Eleven headquarters hadn't yet envisioned a system that could capture online all the movement of individual items at each store, on a daily basis much less minute-by-minute.

Graphic Display Computer / New POS Terminals (1985)

It wasn't until the next round of innovation that Seven-Eleven made full use of its information technology. That was in 1985, when the company introduced its Graphic Display Computer to stores. Certainly this computer and a new POS system the company subsequently introduced marked the dawn of a new era in the use of information technology at Seven-Eleven, but it also added a page to the history of distribution and commerce in Japan.

The launch of the new system coincided also with the company's introduction of an innovative communication system: This new system connected all the 7-Eleven stores via a bi-directional public-line network. Connected to this communication network were 16-bit terminals called Graphic Display Computers. The computers could provide information helpful in the revitalization of business on a store-by-store basis, by leveraging data input through its own POS terminal.

The terminal opened up a new realm of possibility for the member stores, which could now be revitalized through store-driven initiatives. A new infrastructure was built, thereby enabling the stores to freely develop new business opportunities whenever they wanted. What's more, several new businesses were introduced to the stores that would have been impossible before, the first of which was an advance sale system for box lunches provided via a special menu included in the terminal. At the same time, the host computer managing orders was switched from the one in Ohio to a mainframe supercomputer managed by Nomura Computer Systems (now Nomura Research Institute) in Japan.

7-Eleven's Hit Product

One of the new business streams opened by the new technology was a payment service for gas, life insurance, public television, motorcycle insurance, Internet purchases and other third-party services. Before 7-Eleven started this service, public utility charges were handled at the service windows of electric and gas companies, or by bill collectors. Nowadays, one will rarely see a bill collector visiting houses.

7-Eleven's payment service for utility bills and catalogue/mail-order purchases has become a 700 billion-yen ($6.1 billion) business. Moreover, this is a "product" growing at a rate of 30 to 40 percent annually.

The work of the bill collectors was inefficient because so few people were at home when they came to visit the residences of single people or dual-career couples. Instead, remittances from banks came into general use. Banks offered not only payment services for public utilities but also for the settlement of catalogue and mail-order purchases. However, this was very inconvenient from the user's perspective. For example, single employees and working couples couldn't visit banks during business hours because the banks usually closed early, and many banks were closed altogether on Saturdays and during holidays. There was also the automatic deduction service. This was convenient for people with considerable amounts of money in the bank, but not for people who didn't have much in savings.

The convenience store payment service for public utility bills, cell phone charges and catalogue/mail-order purchases was a new opportunity for Seven-Eleven.

Test service of the new POS terminals commenced in June 1985 at a limited number of stores, and the new system went into operation at all 2,700 stores in April of 1986. This was only four years after the first POS system had been installed, reflecting the commitment to investing in innovation. It cost a considerable amount of money to replace the earlier machines with new ones, especially since the older terminals had not been fully depreciated. Member stores were not expected to supply the money for such an endeavor. Indeed, Seven-Eleven bore the entire investment and leased the equipment to its stores.

> *"In our business, information is the breadwinner, so we mustn't be stingy about investing in it."* **—T. Suzuki**

The new, multifunction POS terminal was no commercially available machine, but rather a custom technology for Seven-Eleven. Unlike the earlier entry-only terminals, the new terminal comprised a register and five-inch CRT display. Each was able to connect via public line to exchange data with the Terminal Controller and the network in real time.

The new POS terminals also provided the capability to record customers in ten categories rather than four:

- 12 years old or less   male / female
- 13 to 18 years old   male / female
- 19 to 29 years old   male / female
- 30 to 49 years old   male / female
- 50 years or above   male / female

Combining this customer-group data with a time stamp and item-specific or category-specific trend made the placement of orders much more accurate than the EOB alone was able to do. Additionally, the new terminal ensured that each store had a detailed picture of its actual business and operating conditions. Prior to a delivery, for example, the store received information from the vendor regarding the necessary receiving procedure. The store could then follow those instructions and receive the delivery with few problems. This helped Seven-Eleven better manage its operations. It also allowed them to start recording delivery times, which was important since late deliveries were starting to become a problem. Efforts in that regard eventually led to a precise 30-minute margin of error in arrival time, particularly with respect to box lunches and other fresh items.

Powerful data management capabilities aside, retailers cannot rely solely on data. Distribution and retail business traditionally depended on intuition and experience. To do business solely on the basis of intuition and experience, however, is too much of a gamble. With data, those who lack experience or intuition can, to a certain extent, narrow their judgment, so that they can more easily hit the target. Data allows those who don't have a gambler's heart to make aggressive decisions. It fortifies the intuition of the person doing the ordering.

But for everyone to be able to use data freely as a weapon in daily operations, it has to be practical and easy to use.

Wielding Data

Underlying the development of technology at Seven-Eleven is the notion that data must be output in such a way that anyone can use it to operate the business. After all, the owners of member stores includes people of different backgrounds and abilities. In addition, there are many housewives and temporary employees working at the stores. Some individuals would get headaches just from looking at a computer screen. Others would prefer not to go near them. But at Seven-Eleven, people are taught to wield data as their weapon. The system has to support them.

Initially, the computer terminal was configured to output only basic data that each store needed to meet the specific needs of customers. Subsequently, menus were added to further process the data for output, and the computer itself was upgraded so that it could provide the stores with more practical business benefits. But if the stores were provided with all that data gathered through the POS system, they would find themselves buried in it. Instead of it being used effectively, this information would tgrigger an overload.

To manage that, Seven-Eleven devoted intensive study to the question of how to output database information in ways that are useful for revitalizing the businesses of member stores.

One answer that emerged was embodied in the Graphic Display Computer. The use of graphical representation makes it easier for those who aren't good with numbers to read and understand the information presented. At the same time, output was were limited to prevent information overload. Initially, it was limited by the fundamental nature of the menus provided, but as users became more aware of the importance and utility of data in daily business and acquired more of the skills needed to use that data, the number of menus increased and the output became more sophisticated.

Accordingly, Seven-Eleven initiated comprehensive training programs in the use of data for its member stores. It became part of the orientation training for new stores, and guidance sessions were held for the existing stores. The same is true at Ito-Yokado. A corporate policy objective at the company in 1986, the first full year after the introduction of the POS system, called for all corporate personnel and store staff to "learn how to use POS data."

"A tool becomes either useful or useless depending on the skill of the person using it."　　　　　　　　　　—*T. Suzuki*

The new system enabled part-timers—a sizable force in the operation of 7-Eleven stores—to enter orders, giving them the benefit of precise automation.

With the introduction of the EOB, the Graphic Display Computer, the switch to the new POS terminal and the establishment of a high-tech communication system as a backbone network for such equipment, Seven-Eleven had acquired all of the basic technology components it needed.

The Third Generation: Aiding the Formulation of Hypothesis (1990)

In 1990, Seven-Eleven began to conceptualize its third generation total information system. In its new effort, the company intended to advance its mechanism for total support even further—including an order support system that could more easily achieve an optimal merchandise assortment—in order to increase business at its member stores and raise their standards of management.

One characteristic of the third generation store information system was the elimination of various earlier terminals and the subsequent introduction of new equipment. Another was the switch from a conventional communication network system to an ISDN (Integrated Services Digital Network) offering much greater speed and capacity.

The EOB terminal was scrapped first. Introduced in its place was a new terminal called a Graphic Order Terminal, or GOT. Also introduced was a new, compact computer terminal—the Store Computer, or SC. The latter replaced the Graphic Display Computer that was used to transmit POS data to the host computer and process information in ways that were useful to in-store sales activities. It also supplanted the Terminal Controller, which was used to store master files at each store. The SC offered all the functionality of these two terminals, yet it also had built-in artificial intelligence.

The new GOT was a tablet computer about the size of a sheet of paper. It could be carried around the neck through an attached strap. On its right side was a built-in keyboard. As with the EOB, the person ordering would take a GOT to the sales floor, stand before each gondola, and check the merchandise conditions. The GOT screen displayed summary information contained in the aforementioned merchandise catalogue and the EOB.

But the GOT had functions that the EOB couldn't hope to match. The GOT's nine-inch screen could also display most of the data that before had to be viewed on the Graphic Display Computer. Therefore, it was no longer necessary to go to the back office to see that more detailed information. The person ordering could check the features and marketability of the item to be ordered, as well as points to note regarding handling, ordering and selling via information on the screen right in the aisle. The GOT could display the past sales trend (four-week movement) for a given item at each store, along with the result of a category-based A-B-C ranking of the item. When placing an order, for example, the person could view the sales trends among soft drinks and oolong teas during different temperatures.

The GOT's on-screen data display system was designed by head-quarters staff after going into the field to study the stores and the kinds of information required by the person ordering so that they could formulate hypotheses or make judgments to ensure optimal orders.

The GOT was all the stores needed to retrieve the depth of information available to improve their accuracy in ordering, and ultimately to find the right products to have in the store to drive business. If a store needed more detailed data, it could always check the merchandise catalogue or bring up data on the computer display, or it could ask the OFC for professional advice.

Seven-Eleven's intention was to provide this support information to enable each store to place orders at the highest level of accuracy. By doing so, the company felt, member support would be improved and corporate activity would increase.

> "As the use of the telephone spread, people became dependent on phone communication and wrote fewer letters. In the same way, the introduction of the GOT will make us depend too much on the terminal. We'll simply stop checking the information conveyed through other channels. Therefore, the information supplied through the GOT must be sufficient in quality as well as quantity. At the same time we must always review other communication channels to make possible a more effective supply of information to the member stores." —**T. Suzuki**

Thus, when Seven-Eleven introduced the GOT as a replacement for the EOB, the company embarked on a sweeping innovation in the system of communicating merchandise information between the Product Department and member stores.

Assume, for example, that a store places orders and receives deliveries three times each week for items in a given category. If an order placed today is to be delivered tomorrow, the person ordering must check the items in stock and make a decision as to whether an order should be placed today or if it can wait until the next order date because there will be sufficient stock until then. Ultimately these difficult decisions determine the accuracy of an order. This in turn is the basis for the optimal merchanding that wins customer satisfaction.

The GOT provided the person ordering with information to help them optimize their own judgment and the advice needed in order to formulate a hypothesis. Later, it provided evidence of how accurately the order met actual demand.

Seeing it from a different perspective, the advanced information system and advanced logistics system that now epitomize the operations of Seven-Eleven could never have been built if the company remained dependent on an automated system of ordering. The new business opportunities the company has explored, based on the business infrastructures we've discussed here, would never have materialized.

Information Sharing for Purposeful, Focused Buying

With the introduction of the GOT Suzuki issued a challenge to Seven-Eleven's headquarters Product Department: "Make sure the information conveyed to the person ordering via the GOT will prove truly effective in the formulation of hypotheses." This request exposed a need to drastically reform the way the Product Department was operating.

Upstream Information Makes the Sale

A soft drink called "Acelora" became a hit item in 1990, and the manufacturer launched a line of candies bearing the same name. Upon the introduction of the Acelora candies, the Product Department at Seven-Eleven's headquarters placed an explanatory statement for the candies in its merchandise catalogue. Reading the statement, Suzuki became enraged. He was angry because it was taken literally from the maker's sales rep, describing the candies as "a healthy food rich in vitamins." This wasn't the kind of information the store could find useful. Information supplied to the store should help the staff, including part-timers and temporaries, understand what type of merchandise a product is. Actually, the candies should have been described as a sister product of the red-hot Acelora drink. That way, the staff could have determined how to sell the candies, for example, adopting a particular sales method or ordering a little more than they normally would. Far too many items fit the description of "a healthy food rich in vitamins." He scolded the headquarters' Product Department admonishing them to clearly state why Seven-Eleven had picked up this item in particular out of the universe of all that was available.

The range of products available today far exceeds what customers themselves can know or have the desire or ability to choose from. To carry a broad range of merchandise without giving it meaning or focus just confuses the customer. As a "purchasing agent" the retailer must exercise his or her own professional judgment to procure the items that will give highest satisfaction and value to customers. To do so, it must gather wide-ranging information, select items and build a rational system of procurement on behalf of the customer.

Such a task would be impossible for any one store, even a 7-Eleven franchise. Therefore, the Product Department at headquarters necessarily renders professional services to the member store. It follows that, if the member store is a purchasing agent for the customer, headquarters must act as a purchasing agent for the store.

Headquarters indeed carries out a preliminary selection process, and by listing recommended items, its stores can make a more focused selection with respect to the market. Guided by the professional advice of headquarters buyers, the member store then makes a final selection from among the pre-selected items, and creates a merchandise mix that suits its individual market needs.

The Product Department, through this important pre-selection process, must analyze various buying issues and ask themselves several questions:

• Why choose this item out of all the things available in the world?
• What's wrong with choosing other items?
• What meaning or value does it provide for the 7-Eleven customer?
• What different value does it have from the customer's viewpoint when compared with items of the same type?
• What will happen to the store if it handles this item?
• Does it offer a differentiation factor from other stores?

- What are the store locations and customer groups that suit this item?
- What result can the store expect from carrying it?

Suzuki calls this analysis "purposeful, focused buying activity" the results of which must be conveyed to stores. It's also precisely the kind of information that the GOT is designed to display. By communicating such information, the headquarters buyer and the person working at the store share a common perspective.

Makoto Usui, a Seven-Eleven Japan board director in charge of information systems, led a system development team of Seven-Eleven staff and outside experts, said of the project: "Behind Seven-Eleven's strong business results lies an effort by each store to eliminate lost opportunities due to out-of-stocks, etc., in order to achieve expanded equilibrium. Crucial to the company's business is the tanpin kanri technique whereby the store places an order by formulating a hypothesis based on the day's weather and its customer trends, and by which it works to improve the accuracy of the next order by verifying the result of past orders with data. In that respect, it's important that the person ordering at each store be able to use information effectively. And from the company perspective, it's necessary to provide an information system that anyone can understand and use, and one that requires the staff to develop a habit of checking information and data."

The Fifth Generation—From Weather Forecasts to TV Ads (2000)

Through the introduction of the Store Computer and GOT terminals, Seven-Eleven's third generation total information system established a support system that dramatically increased the accuracy of ordering at member stores by helping them hypothesize and verify results in daily operations. The stores could actively implement business strategies designed to ensure high customer satisfaction and value.

The Winter 1997 edition of the "Ito-Yokado Group Quarterly Report" newsletter featured an article introducing Seven-Eleven's fifth generation total information system. In part, the article reads as follows: "One trademark of information system development at Seven-Eleven is that the primary focus is given to the need for information that arises in day-to-day work, such as what kind of information is required for an accurate hypothesis and what type of mechanism is required to share and use information. The information system is conceptualized based on these needs and a clear policy is set forth by Seven-Eleven. Then, technological development and system building slowly commence in collaboration with experts."

Characteristics of the Fifth Generation System
- A communications satellite-linked ISDN that is among the largest in the world
- Full-scale utilization of multimedia technology, including image and voice via in-store computers and GOT.
- One mobile personal computer each for approximately 1,500 OFCs and other front-line sales staff
- Full migration to an open architecture offering flexibility, expandability and unrestricted connectivity
- Improved reliability, maintenance and serviceability through the joint development of dedicated hardware and software (Seven-Eleven outsources software and hardware development from a group of 12 collaborating companies, including Nomura Research Institute and NEC.)

Usui recalls the company's need for this new system, as follows: "We wanted the person ordering to learn from commercials that were running on TV. The most effective way to do this was to show them the commercials ourselves. This led to the idea of adding a button to retrieve and display video on the screen of the order terminal (GOT). Moreover, we wanted to display video and images showing how to sell each item, and how to recommend it to customers so as to help the store staff understand the correct approach. We also looked into utilizing voice and hand-written text for store communication."

In order to satisfy these needs, the company had to incorporate multimedia functionality. The decision to use a digital communications satellite came about from the need to transmit vast amounts of image and text data. Seven-Eleven decided to use, without further modification, the communication system it was already using to transmit promotional video for game titles to a TV monitor installed in each store. A store information system capable of providing video, still images, text and numerical data was introduced franchise-wide in April 1998.

The system is designed to facilitate accurate ordering based on hypothesis by enabling the person ordering to check not only the POS data of each item but also weather information, local events that might impact the demand for that item, the item's current promotional campaign, and so on.

Prior to the system's introduction, product information and local weather information were being supplied separately to the store, the former through photo catalogues and the latter through a dedicated weather-information system. This new system combined these two types of information, thereby allowing the person ordering to review all of the detailed information on the GOT screen with just a click of a button. The graphical system made physical merchandise catalogues and order books obsolete, reducing the consumption of paper by as much as 73 million pages annually.

In 1992, as part of the third generation system, Seven-Eleven's organization has employed an ISDN capable of transmitting large volumes of data simultaneously. But even a network that powerful couldn't offer sufficient transmission capacity when it came to sending many bytes of video and still-image data. So the fifth generation total information system employs both channels—the new network system linked via ISDN and the digital communications satellite, making this system among the largest of its kind in the world. The dual system is able to transmit 3 terabytes of data every month. It transmits everything—even in-store audio programming.

The new network offers a communication speed 45 times greater and a cost performance 35 times greater than the level achieved by the dedicated ISDN network alone. Moreover, the network makes it possible to centrally manage and update the master files, programs and operating software housed in all the 50,000 plus terminals throughout the network.

The increased data processing speed is in fact what made it possible to extend the deadline for orders from 10 a.m. to 11 a.m. It did so without affecting the supplier's order-data upload time or delivery time to the store and allows extra time for working on order placement. Furthermore, the availability of to-the-minute sales data and weather information provided a basis for even further improvement in order accuracy.

Vendors are also provided advanced sytems for order placement and acceptance. For instance, suppliers of box lunches and the like make use of a total information system that encompasses every step of the process, from material procurement and production control to shipping. Systems for combined distribution centers also offer enhanced support functions for inventory control and other processes, thereby enabling the staff involved with separate processes—from material procurement and production to distribution and sale—to share information and achieve greater uniformity of effort.

And in the area of store support, each of the OFC and other front-line sales staff carry a mobile personal computer so that they can easily check order information, POS data and the like wherever they might go. This enables the OFC to give timely advice and support to each store under his or her watch.

Finally, subsequent to the introduction of these operational systems, the POS information system and in-store POS register system were also upgraded to new systems. The new POS information system can perform a range of analyses to identify relationships between the movement of each item and the weather, local events and so on.

Support by OFCs as Information Commentators

Seven-Eleven maintains a team of operation field counselors (OFCs). They're front-line soldiers assigned to the territories managed by a corporate headquarters. Each OFC is responsible for an average of seven or eight stores, providing them with consultation as part of headquarters' total support activities. In fact, more than 1,000 personnel—including OFCs and their supervising district managers—are now functioning as consultants to assist the local member stores in boosting their sales.

The OFCs must visit each of their stores at least twice a week, and spend at least three hours at each visit. The OFCs check the operating conditions of member stores with which they're charged, but they do so by observing the operations of stores from a customer's point of view. Needless to say, the primary goal of the OFCs here is not policing but to revitalize their stores' sales activity by helping them maintain an optimal assortment of merchandise in stock. Their primary task is to help the member store do a job that should essentially be done by the store itself; that is, to analyze the operation "self-objectively" or, to put it simply, as the customer would. Stores that are immersed in everyday activities tend not to be able to see themselves through the impartial, objective and detached eyes of a third party. It's important, therefore, that the OFCs do this for them.

An equally important responsibility of the OFCs is to help headquarters see itself objectively; to allow headquarters to check its support activities for the member stores and evaluate whether it's really effective in helping them run their business better. In other words, the OFCs check headquarters' operations objectively, from the standpoint of a member store.

To make this consulting activity more fruitful, it's ideal that the OFCs spend as much time as possible with each store and provide comprehensive assistance. That's why one OFC is in charge of just seven or eight stores.

The OFC makes specific suggestions related to the various data and information sent to the store via the information communication network. For example, he or she might say to the owner of a store, "The data shows that this item has often been out-of-stock lately. Business-wise, you're losing this much money from opportunity loss. Since this other item has been selling particularly well lately for such-and-such reasons, I suggest you take a positive stance and place a slightly more aggressive order." To enhance such advice, each OFC has a mobile personal computer designed exclusively for Seven-Eleven. With this computer he or she can quickly retrieve support data for use in the visit. At the weekly OFC conference mentioned in Chapter 1, the OFCs receive information and detailed explanations from specialists in various fields within corporate departments.

The Seven-Eleven system of information sharing is one that the company has constantly refined since the first days of its establishment. It doesn't consist merely of lifeless computers and digital communication systems. In addition to cutting edge technology Seven-Eleven understands the importance of human interaction—"humanware"—as a key component of the innovative systems of information it creates.

Chapter 8

The Goal: Grasping Customer Demand

S uzuki constantly preaches the following.

"Take your time when placing an order."   —*T. Suzuki*

The massive investment in Seven-Eleven's fifth generation system is actually devoted to this somewhat simple directive.

A minimum lead-time is inherent in production and processing. To arbitrarily reduce the production/processing time would affect quality and eventually add to cost. Ideally, the production/processing and delivery schedule should be as close as possible to the moment of consumption. Accordingly, the lead-time from the moment an order is placed until the item is produced and delivered must be as short as possible. The system revolution that Seven-Eleven has been implementing aims at reducing this lead-time and eliminating the discrepancies that exist between production and sales—in terms of time, physical distance and feelings.

Logically, being able to order on the same day products are to be delivered certainly allows a retailer to respond to actual conditions better than if they had to place orders a day in advance. One could, for example, place an order assuming that the next day's weather will be fine, only to wake up in a downpour. Such an inaccuracy in ordering creates discrepancies between the production, warehousing or delivery and true demand.

One improvement to the process has made it possible, for example, to push back the order deadline for box lunches and prepared foods by one whole hour. Even when ordering in the morning, it's better to place an order at 11 o'clock than 10 o'clock. With an extra hour available, the store can more accurately grasp the actual conditions of its individual market, which of course are subject to constant change. If used wisely, that extra hour allows the staff to take more time placing orders (making decisions). That is, put more care into formulating a hypothesis.

Seven-Eleven has spent a considerable sum of money for such things as a system that allows the person ordering to bring up a weather forecast in a corner of the screen of the GOT terminal. He/she can also view a corresponding TV commercial and a variety of other information regarding an item.

It isn't impossible to and ask hardware and software companies to build these same functions provided that you have enough money. However, the purpose of developing such a system or technology isn't to satisfy an engineer's curiosity or the pride of management. Unless the field staff can operate and use it to yield a specific outcome, a system or technology will be practically and economically useless. Therefore, it's essential that the store has a clear understanding and awareness as to why such technology or mechanism is needed.

Basically, every system should be designed to assist each store in its effort to run business in ways that answer customer needs. But in actuality, many retailers are little aware of the importance of it; they don't see how understanding demand could affect their business.

Seven-Eleven pursued system innovation in order to build an infrastructure—a support system—that would improve the efficiency of hypothesis and verification at each store. This system would be useless for any other business that didn't share the same vision.

An information system doesn't simply mean the conveyance of POS data from downstream to upstream. I've repeatedly mentioned in this book that numbers indicating how much of which item has sold are just data, not information. As is summarized in the phrase, "We don't place an order because a product has sold well, we place the order because we believe the product will sell well," the idea of "ordering for replenishment" should be refuted.

Grasping Customer Demand

Seven-Eleven Japan invested a total of 60 billion yen ($522 million) in its fifth generation total information system alone. Remember that the company had already spent considerable sums in the development of its first, third and fourth generation systems as well. The investment deserves particular note, partly because of its magnitude—60 billion yen is equivalent to the annual sales of a leading local retail chain, and partly because the money isn't directed toward the building or improvement of stores; instead, the money was devoted to the creation of an infrastructure to support the corporate philosophy behind the scenes.

Nearly every company active in the distribution/commerce industry (including retailers and restaurants) has directed most of their investment toward building or renovating stores. Everyone seems to think that the distribution/commerce industry will weaken and decline if it neglects the scrap-and-build approach toward better locations and larger spaces. However, Seven-Eleven has achieved remarkable growth without relying exclusively on increasing space.

Instead of capital investment in buildings and physical things, Seven-Eleven has been throwing money at technology. Specifically, the company is driven toward innovation relating to merchandise, merchandise assortments, service, the sales system and various operational systems that support them (including systems relating to distribution/logistics, information system and store operation/management). It's a total management system that integrates all of those components.

The drive toward innovation centered on information systems is widely considered to be the key to Seven-Eleven's success today. Of course, these huge investments wouldn't be possible without the company's remarkable profits, amounting to 140 billion yen ($1.2 billion) for the fiscal year 2000 sales. Compared to the previous year, it was a 112 percent jump. Indeed, such a massive investment in technology may be Seven-Eleven's answer to the criticism that the company is making too much money.

"In the beginning," Suzuki said, "there were many criticisms that Seven-Eleven's franchise fee (money paid by the member stores to the head office in return for support) was too high, the rate being 45 percent of the gross margin. People also pointed out that the head office was recording large profits and criticized us by saying we were making too much money. But this profit all became an essential source of funds for our investment in innovation."

In a sense, the relationship between success and investment is very much like the proverbial relationship between the chicken and the egg: Which comes first?

The first retailer to become a 7-Eleven member store was the Yamamoto Liquor Store located in the Toyosu neighborhood of Tokyo. When this first franchise store opened over 25 years ago, the 100-square-meter business was generating under 400,000 yen ($3,478) per day. It was the only full-scale convenience chain store in the area. Following its debut, rival convenience stores emerged at nearby locations, one after another. Despite this competition, the store currently generates more than 2.5 million yen ($21,739) a day from the exact same floor space.

In case you're thinking the success of that store has come about merely by accident. Such growth is not unusual in the 7-Eleven network. The average daily sales of all 7-Eleven stores in Japan was 380,500 yen ($3,309) in 1976. Today, the average daily sales have increased substantially to around 700,000 yen ($6,087), That is proof of the power of the tanpin kanri approach.

Responding to Change

Commitment to technology and changing with the times is the hallmark of Seven-Eleven.

> *"An increase in the number of stores from 1,000 to 2,000 doesn't simply mean the quality of the system should also be doubled. In fact, the required system quality increases exponentially, by a multiple of ten. In that sense, to blindly increase the scale without innovation will only create drawbacks. True economy of scale is realized only when such drawbacks are eliminated."*
> —*T. Suzuki*

Seven-Eleven has consistently used the scrap-and-build approach toward excellence, engaging in endless rounds of software innovation. The company's commitment in this regard is perhaps stronger than any other company in Japan's distribution industry. And true to that commitment, the company is resolutely and indefatigably maintaining a strategic decision to allocate tangible and intangible management resources to this purpose. This is ample evidence that the company has a clear vision of its being and ultimately its growth.

It's only natural that a business relying on software for its existence would choose a path of unending innovation and creative destruction—a scrap-and-build approach where software is concerned. This is a company that functions not by maintaining and owning the means of material production such as hardware, but by "using" it. This philosophy is also reflected in Seven-Eleven's commitment to outsourcing.

"The only thing a company can rely on is innovation," says Suzuki. He often points to macro-level changes in the world and bases his management on a process of responding to change. To respond to change, one must innovate, and to innovate is to have wisdom on which one can act. So in this time of change, Suzuki's management attaches primary importance to knowledge.

"You can rationalize and save other costs and expenses, but you should never spare investment in communication and infor-mation." **—T. Suzuki**

Information comes in various forms, but it goes without saying that the most important information a company can have relates to the individual and specific needs of the customer. A store's or a company's existence and survival, not to mention its growth and prosperity, depend on whether it can win the support of the market and the customer. Sales are the result of that support, and the way to win it is to provide satisfaction, value and worthiness.

Companies are learning the painful lessons of this rule in today's dynamic buyer's market. Companies that deviate from this rule will be weeded out regardless of their size, industry, or type of trade or operation. To ensure customer satisfaction, value and worthiness, companies must first "grasp the customer." They need to view all their actions from the customer's perspective. The importance of "grasping the customer" in the retail industry doesn't apply to store operations exclusively. It's a universal condition for all processes contributing to the achievement of an optimal mix at the store, including production, delivery, merchandise procurement, development, etc.

In May of 1999, I had a chance to watch a video created for an association of Ito-Yokado's dealers; it described clothing sales at Ito-Yokado. Of the 20 best-selling women's blouses, 16 items (80 percent of the total) represented a new color, pattern, material, design, etc. that hadn't been seen in the previous season. In the buyer's market, customer's needs are changing quickly and dramatically. They're becoming more selective. In that sense, the target is getting smaller and moving constantly amid the darkness. Without a steady and accurate aim, the arrow will miss the target.

In the buyer's market, there are many companies that still can't see the customer, and they find themselves challenged to deliver profits. It isn't enough simply to have production facilities, distribution equipment, stores and sales floors. Unless a company has the means and know-how regarding what to make, in which way, in what quantity and through which means to deliver, purchase, stock and sell its products, that company won't see great returns. Without this kind of knowledge, it won't matter how much manpower, physical resources and money they have available. All that counts is grasping the customer's individual and specific needs.

Thus we come to the conclusion that what drives production, delivery, procurement and sales in a challenging buyer's market is information that allows a company to "grasp the customer." Retailers who want to survive must become enthusiastic users of any and all information that helps them do this. Seven-Eleven has emphasized this concept more than anyone else and has sincerely devoted itself strategically and tactically to enabling this process.

The company's 60-billion-yen investment in its fifth generation total information system was founded on a desire to build a system with which to "grasp the customer," one that would facilitate the process of hypothesis and verification and ensure accuracy in ordering. Yet the system the company pursues is of a decidedly greater dimension. It's one that allows manufacturers and wholesalers to share accurate orders as truth; one that allows the company to practice production/delivery based on information sharing, and to procure optimal items in optimal quantities at optimal timing under optimal conditions from the customer's viewpoint; and one that leads directly to innovation in logistics and merchandising reform. In the end, it results in development of products that keep customers coming back for more.

About the Author:

Tomoyuki Ogata has been writing and editing about the distribution industry since 1964. Early in his career he spent 14 years as chief editor of "Hanbai Kakushin," a trade magazine for the chain store industry published by Shogyokai. He later came to oversee five monthly magazines there. In 1983, he established Office 2020, which publishes the distribution industry monthly "2020 AIM" and several books on Japanese distribution industry issues. He is well known for tracking the rapid paradigm shifts that occur with ongoing innovation in the information-oriented society and for his attempts to define the new roles that are required of the retail and distribution industry. He is a well-respected lecturer and author of some 30 books, a select bibliography of which follows.

— *Tanpin Kanri (Tanpin Kanri: Evolutionary Theory of Seven-Eleven Japan's IT Strategy)* East Press, Sep. 2000

— *Askul (Askul: A Company Evolving with Customers)* PHP Interface, Feb. 2001

— *Futari no Ryutsu Kakumei (Distribution Revolution by Two Leaders: Isao Nakauchi and Toshifumi Suzuki)*; Nikkei Business Publications, Jul. 1999

— *Okyaku wo Erabe (Select Your Customer: Transforming from a "Number 1" Strategy to an "Only One" Strategy)*; Diamond Inc., Aug. 1998

— *The Syouninjuku (Lessons for Merchants: What are the Requirement for Merchants following the Big Bang of Distribution?)*; OS Publishing, Apr. 1998

— *Syaddy Kando Souzou No Keiei (Syaddy, Its Management Style of Soul Stirring Creation)*; Office 2020, Jan. 1996

— *Ito Yokado no Gyoukaku Part 3 (Business Revolution of Ito Yokado Part3: Challenge to Merchandising Revolution)*; Office 2020, Aug. 1992

— *Daiei ga Yomigaeru Toki (Daiei's Revival)*; Office 2020, Dec. 1985

— *Jusco no Keiei (Jusco's Management Style)*; Nippon Jitsugyo Publishing, Dec. 1978

About the Editor:

Daniel Costello is a freelance writer and the author of dozens of recent articles on business strategy and the application of technology. A former market researcher and consultant, he specializes in issues relating to customer relationship management (CRM); marketing automation; knowledge management; retail strategy; and the consumer packaged goods industry. Mr. Costello has worked with many of the largest companies in the United States and Japan across a wide range of industries. He speaks and reads Japanese fluently.